ANTHRACITE GRADE SCHOOL

On Irish Hill

Helen,

Thank you, and
Good Luck!

Sonny Ronald Scatena
May 23, 2015

ANTHRACITE GRADE SCHOOL
On Irish Hill

Louis Ronald Scatena

TATE PUBLISHING
AND ENTERPRISES, LLC

Published by Tate Publishing & Enterprises, LLC
127 E. Trade Center Terrace | Mustang, Oklahoma 73064 USA
1.888.361.9473 | www.tatepublishing.com

Tate Publishing is committed to excellence in the publishing industry. The company reflects the philosophy established by the founders, based on Psalm 68:11,
"The Lord gave the word and great was the company of those who published it."

Book design copyright © 2014 by Tate Publishing, LLC. All rights reserved.
Cover design by Carlo Nino Suico
Interior design by Honeylette Pino

Published in the United States of America

ISBN: 978-1-63268-275-8
History / North America
14.07.01

This story is about my father and anthracite coal mining and is dedicated to my mother, Caroline, who to this day, never waivered in her devotion to her principles. By example and with a subtle pride based on her own personal unwritten code, she taught Linda, Carol, and I the true meaning of honor under any circumstances of personal hardship. In the context of her life, honor is defined as, "Always taking the path in support of family, friends, and country, as God intended, and without any deviation in that path for personal gain." This story is Mother's, as much as it is my own.

CONTENTS

PREFACE

This is a story of men struggling in a black underground world as they and their families emerge from a very difficult period of industrial labor strife and economic depression. It is also a story of a father's effort to school a young boy to work with a passion that he felt was necessary to a successful life. This story is not about coal mining in the veins where they are deep, thick, and overlain by many feet of solid rock. It's not about miners at major collieries who entered on cable cars down a shaft or slope or stood erect in high underground rooms such as were often portrayed in such classic films about coal mining as *How Green Was My Valley*, *The Molly Maguires*, or on public television. Certainly, those miners persevered in a monumentally hazardous environment that is well documented.

Instead, this story is about anthracite mining along the mountainsides where the veins approach the surface—i.e., where the veins outcrop. Here veins and rock cover are thin, anthracite is softer, and roof rock, more often than not, is extensively fractured. Veins may only be three to five feet thick, dip, turn, twist, abruptly terminate, resume a short distance away, and cannot often be identified accurately by name or on mine maps. All of the safety issues that confronted miners in the large collieries were multiplied at these mines near the outcrops. State and federal inspectors also visited these small operations, but most likely, not with the frequency and enthusiasm focused on larger operations where the majority of anthracite miners were at risk. For all of these reasons, miners commonly nicknamed these ominous-looking mine openings that once dotted the mountainsides of the anthracite fields as dogholes. Classic stories about mines tell of warnings rats provided by running out of a mine just prior to a cave-in. During my youthful experience around dogholes from 1951 to 1959, I never heard that any rats were seen. The rats probably took one look and decided to migrate elsewhere.

This story is also about my schooling in those years, from the age of nine to seventeen, in such mining operations with my father in Northeastern Pennsylvania—specifically, the region between Scranton and Wilkes-Barre known as the Wyoming Valley. A portion of the Valley appears in figure 1. The story begins in chapters 1 and 2 with a description of the hardships that prevailed in the anthracite fields at the time immigration was at its peak, and chapter 3 describes the struggle for survival a little later during the Great Depression. It is only with the background knowledge of previous hardship that one can truly understand the motives of the generation of anthracite miners that followed in chapters 4 through 12, including my father and the doghole miners who are the primary subject of this account of life around the mines. It would be grossly misleading and unfair to judge their actions in the context of life as we now know it.

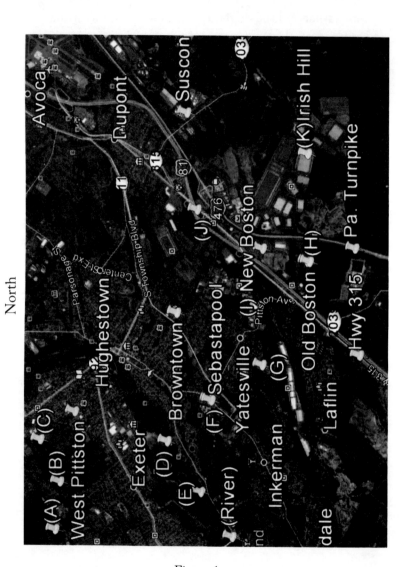

Figure 1

CHAPTER I

THE ANTHRACITE REVOLUTION (1897-1903)

In 1900, there were approximately 150,000 miners in the anthracite coalfields centered around the Northeastern Pennsylvania towns of Scranton, Wilkes-Barre, and Pottsville. The production of anthracite not only fueled homes, but even more importantly, the development of the steel and other related industries to the point where the United States began to surpass Great Britain as the industrial capital of the world. But the wealth was accumulated by powerful industrialists at the expense of immigrants from Europe who sacrificed their blood, sweat, and tears after they read the enticing advertisements (by the industrialists) of the wealth possible in America. Compared to the famine that existed in their own native country, they were induced to beg and borrow the money needed to cover the cost of immigration. Once here, however, the miners soon realized that their participation in the wealth was only imagined. Industrialists created a network of six railroads in the northeastern United States in a concerted effort to control anthracite sales, prices, and wages, and publicized union members as destabilizing socialists. As the owners of the steel plants, railroads, banks, and other industries planned it, an annual income of 400-500 dollars was just enough to put bread and potatoes on a miner's plate to sustain his return to the colliery each day. Miners and their families often lived in shacks adjacent to the colliery and paid rent to mine operators. Mothers shopped at the company store where they were forced to pay the high prices because it was the only shop where they could buy on credit as long as their underpaid husbands continued to mine coal. Tennessee Ernie Ford summed up the miners' plight in his hit song "Sixteen Tons," when he sang, "St. Peter don't you take me cause I can't go. I owe my soul to the company store."

As might be imagined, many industrialists and their railroad subsidiaries wanted to keep unions out and had little regard for mine safety. On average, one anthracite miner was killed in a mine accident every day. In 1901, 513 anthracite miners were killed and more than 10,000 seriously injured. Industrialists also hired private security forces to help control miners who demonstrated. In 1897, a large group of miners peacefully demonstrated near Hazleton, and nineteen were shot and killed by such a so-called security force. (1)

A series of prolonged strikes by anthracite miners between 1900 and 1902 resulted in a national fuel crisis during which President Theodore Roosevelt created an Arbitration Commission. The Commission began to listen to testimony by miners and mine operators at the Lackawanna County Courthouse in Scranton in November 1902. John Mitchell of the fledgling United Mine Workers of America was interviewed for five days. He hired the renowned socialist lawyer, Clarence Darrow, to facilitate testimony by miners for about six weeks. In January and February of 1903, owners testified and accused demonstrating miners of destroying mine property and attacking scabs—the miners' nickname for the 20,000 destitute miners who continued to work during the strike. In March of 1903, the Presidential Commission ruled that wages must be increased 10 percent, the wage must be based on each ton mined, the coal must be weighed fairly, and wages should rise as coal prices increase. (1)

President Roosevelt was sincere in his effort to help the miners, but he was also compelled to revive the industry from the strike that had crippled the nation and the Commission also ruled that miners must return to work. Despite the efforts of the president's Commission, the efforts of the fledgling United Mine Workers under John Mitchell, and the eloquent rhetoric of Clarence Darrow, only partial improvements occurred. If a miner received ten dollars per week previously, he now received eleven, and the company store would likely find a way to recover all or part of the additional dollar. The plight of the Anthracite miners would continue for thirty to thirty-five years as the United Mine Workers under John L. Lewis fought to gradually receive and implement meaningful wage, health, and retirement programs. Perhaps the strike's most significant benefit was that more than previously, the miners now had a recognized voice in the American labor industry.

My grandfather immigrated to that difficult environment from Spoleto in north central Italy in 1908, where he had worked in the lignite coal mines. He obviously hoped to participate in the wealth of anthracite mining at a colliery near the town of Plains, just north of Wilkes-Barre. Years ago, I had heard how my grandfather (Nonno), who died the year before I was born, was a staunch supporter of the Mine Worker's Union and why he often found it necessary to carry a pistol and/or blackjack to defend himself. My father-in-Law, Pete, immigrated from Scheggia in North Central Italy in 1928 at age sixteen to work in an anthracite colliery near Jessup, just north of Scranton. Many years later, Pete described to me how he disembarked with tears of happiness at Ellis Island in 1928 as the ship's public address system blared the sentimental music of "La Vien Rose." Big Pete, as fellow miners called him, sadly recounted the grave conditions that he soon encountered in the collieries and his many battles with mine owners and scabs. Just like Nonno, he, too, was a staunch, outspoken member of the Mine Workers' Union. Unable to afford anything more sophisticated at that time, he described how bricks could be thrown far and accurately after banging two together to form smaller baseball-sized missiles. So despondent had he become over the lack of opportunity in 1929, he considered returning to Italy, but could not with the stark realization that his parents had committed all of their financial resources to send him to America.

Thirty years after immigration, Big Pete had worked his way to a position of partnership in one of the largest and most productive mines in Scranton: The Diamond Colliery. From 1900 to 1940, however, such success was hardly a dream among anthracite miners.

CHAPTER II

IMMIGRATION (1904-1915)

Nonna's first husband immigrated from Gualdo, Italy, to work in a colliery in the Old Boston Settlement around 1913, leaving Nonna, Uncle Ted, Aunt Della, and Aunt Vienna behind until such time as he was able to send for them. The Settlement is approximately eight miles north of Wilkes-Barre, on the east side of Highway 315 (near bottom of figure 1). His plan was obviously on track in 1914 because by then he had purchased a small home or shack about 300 feet down the road and south of the Old Boston Italian Citizen's Club. The club still stands today, and I have fond memories of the many evenings Dad took me there in the 1950s to observe the miners playing bocce, darts, shuffleboard, card games, and morra. The most exciting events occurred when the bocce team played other miners from similar clubs in Plains, Hudson, Keystone, Browntown (near center of figure 1), and other anthracite mining communities in an organized Bocce League.

The 1915 Wilkes-Barre Record Almanac reports that there were fourteen homicides in Luzerne County in 1914. Although his alleged indiscretion was later disproved, it said of Nonna's first husband, "In November Luigi Corsaletti of Boston Settlement was shot by a boarding house keeper for alleged intimacy with the latter's wife." With the encouragement of her sister, Adele, who had already immigrated to the nearby town of Plains, Nonna, Uncle Ted, and Aunt Vienna immigrated to Old Boston in 1915 to live in the house left by her deceased first husband. Aunt Della was left behind in Gualdo to live with Nonna's mother because Nonna felt it would be impossible to safely manage the three children during the long voyage. Nonna's sister wrote also that Nonna would have a wonderful opportunity to wed a very nice hardworking miner who was a personal friend to Adele and Adele's husband. Of course, Adele was referring to my grandfather, Nonno.

Nonno was born in 1884 and was one of 800 to 900 men who worked in the large, state-of-the-art lignite mines near Spoleto, Italy. Lignite coal contains less carbon and produces less fuel than bituminous or anthracite. Nonno's father, Bernardino, also worked at the mine. The lignite was used to fuel the foundries in the larger industrial city of Terni, eighteen miles to the south of Spoleto. The mines opened in 1880 and the miners were under the oppressive control of industrialists based in Terni. Almost as if they had taken their cue from fellow miners in Northeastern Pennsylvania, the miners in Spoleto went on prolonged strikes in 1906 and 1907 to protest very dangerous working conditions and low wages. In 1907, the newspaper *Giovanne Umbria* wrote that Terni industrialists agreed to augment salary, "Ma non a tutti, a chi merita," which translated said, "But not for every miner; only those who merit it." The League of Miners responded, "This plan is unacceptable because it will create favoritism, jealousy, and discontent." The newspaper then reported, "This plan is a delusion and is unsatisfactory. Now begins a period of difficult agitation."

More than likely, these political and economic conditions were at the root of Nonno's decision, and the decision of thousands of European miners, to immigrate to Northeastern Pennsylvania. According to immigration records available in the vast genealogical libraries of the Mormon Church in Salt Lake City, Nonno departed Naples, Italy, on August 29, 1908, on the SS *Cretic* and arrived at Ellis Island in New York on September 11. In the ship's manifest, Nonno reported that he was twenty-four years old, single, could read/write, and had $24 in his possession. After seeing the quality of his personal signature on a "Petition for Naturalization" dated September 17, 1917, it raised a question whether Nonno could indeed write. In one column of the ship's manifest, each immigrant had to report his occupation. On line after line, page after page, men said, "Laborer," but Nonno said, "Miner." It suggested to me that Nonno and other miners were proud to make that distinction. An historical account titled "Le Miniere di Lignite di Spoleto" stated the League of Miners was a proud fraternity. In the preface, Giovanni Antonelli writes that the miners were an unusual hardworking breed, with strength and character, and born with a resolve to endure hardship. The book's author writes that the proud League hired artists to fabricate bronze statues of their leaders and heroes throughout the coalfields and to design a colorful organizational flag. They also designated a special holiday called the Feast of St. Barbara, which they celebrated each year with a very large festival on December 4. (2)

The miners of Northeastern Pennsylvania brought this strong sense of pride with them from Europe and passed it on to their descendents. Indeed, the fraternity of miners of Northeastern Pennsylvania celebrated John Mitchell Day on October 29. Many miners also looked forward to the annual John Kehoe Celebration at the coal magnate's estate in Harding, just up the Susquehanna River a few miles from Pittston (figure 1). With pride in its heritage, the City of Scranton built the Anthracite Museum in West Scranton. With similar pride, a museum has also been dedicated to the lignite miners at the shaft where Nonno and his father once worked in the small village of Morgnano, just outside Spoleto. The people, pride, perseverance, and politics of miners in Europe and Northeastern Pennsylvania were the same, separated only by the Atlantic Ocean.

The following story of Nonna's first meeting with Nonno in 1915 in the mining settlement of Old Boston was described to me by Aunt Della, many years after Nonna had summarized it for my aunt:

> When Nonna entered the room where she knew she was about to meet her future husband for

the first time, more than a dozen miners were seated around the room in their best Sunday outfits. Very self-conscious and nervous, Nonna glanced around the room out of the corner of her eye and one man, in particular, caught her attention. Nonna recalled that he had a robust, healthy complexion, well-groomed mustache, and a meticulous black suit, vest, tie, and trousers tucked in wide leather straps that wrapped the top of his shining black boots. Nonna avoided eye contact with him and recalled telling herself, *No, it can't be. I'm not that lucky!* She also sensed out of the corner of her eye that he was intently observing her every move. Then, as the other well-groomed miners seated against the walls passed a wine jug from one miner to the next, the man next to Nonno asked him if he wanted a drink, referring to him by name. At that instant, Nonna lost her breath and recalled that Nonno replied, "No graci," and passed the jug to the man on his other side without taking his eyes off Nonna.

> Aunt Della Musto, during a visit
> to her home in Hughestown in 1987

Immigrant miners very likely had a strong preference to marry a woman from their native country, and Nonna's somewhat steamy account is only one example of the many transatlantic arranged marriages of that period and the circumstances leading to the next generation of anthracite miners. As with other immigrants of that period, however, Nonna would soon realize that her luck was prematurely imagined.

CHAPTER III

DESPERATION AND THE GREAT DEPRESSION (1916-1939)

Aunt Della recalled for me how she cried in 1915 at age four as she watched her mother, brother Dorato (Uncle Ted), and sister Vienna ride away in horse and buggy to the train station. She desperately reached for the rear of the buggy as tearful relatives restrained her. Aunt Della said she refused to eat for many days and became ill. It strikes me as a little odd that Aunt Della could remember so many details from the age of four, and it may be possible that she was recounting details shared over time by older relatives. It was not until 1922 at age eleven that her mother and stepfather sent for her. Aunt Della traveled to America with her aunt, who was also immigrating to rejoin her coal miner husband near Pittston. Once settled in Old Boston for a few months, Aunt Della said life was so hard, even six or seven years prior to the onset of the Great Depression, that she wished she could return to her grandmother in Gualdo. She said she felt that the primary reason she had been summoned from Italy was to assist Nonna with housework and look after her sisters and brothers. "She felt" are the key words here because Aunt Della (and I) sincerely doubted this was her mother's true motive. By this time, however, Nonna now had six children to care for, with more to come. So great was the demand for Aunt Della's domestic services that Nonno refused to let her go to elementary school. When the truant officer paid a visit, Nonno would give him a few glasses of homemade red wine, a gallon of the freshly squeezed variety to take home, and a sad plea that the household was enduring too much hardship to spare Aunt Della for grade school. Nonna's dilemma at the time can only be imagined. She also had to endure the birth of four more children between 1922 and 1932, but through seldom spoken innuendo, I learned that Nonna also self-aborted on four other occasions. Apparently, during the Depression, some forlorn women used a method involving extremely hot bathwater soon after conception. I distinctly recall Nonna's tenderness toward her ten children or "my chillee" as she referred to them while struggling with the language and understand why she felt compelled to take such drastic measures during those very difficult years.

From 1915 to 1940, the family endured, grew, and evolved, often with the help of kind neighbors. For example, a thoughtful mailman kept an eye open for discarded clothing and would distribute it among the homeowners, including Nonno and Nonna. As with all mining families of the time, Nonna and her daughters did their best to stitch clothing from whatever cloth was available, including sacks that previously were filled with baking flour. Mother said flour sacks were also put to such use in her own home when she was a child. On one occasion, when her older sister bought a slip at a store, her father complained in broken English, "Holly Wuud?" He felt such extravagant clothing was only worn by movie stars.

During the Great Depression, the demand for coal and miners was very weak. To make matters worse, Nonno's outspoken defense of the mineworkers union weakened his opportunity on the few days that mine superintendents selected from the pool of candidates gathered near the entrance to the mine. In this critical time of need, the family had to rely on every possible means of placing food on the table. Some of the younger children began going to elementary school, but before walking three miles from Old Boston to the school in Sebastapool (Location F in figure 1), south of Pittston, it was mandatory that they till and maintain the vegetable gardens that were planted on three sides of the home. Hunger was relatively uncommon, provided no one disliked the food that was made available. In the summer, Nonna often led her children into the hills east of Old Boston to pick buckets of blueberries. The berries were not used to make pies, but were bottled and placed later on fresh (or stale) bread for the morning's breakfast. Wild dandelions were picked wherever they grew and served as dinner salad. In the fall, mushrooms also became available.

It is doubtful there were large flocks of robins or sparrows around Old Boston in those years. Dad and his friend, Sam, once recounted how their fathers would roast these on an open fire after removing the feathers. However, the young boys were reluctant to eat beyond the surface flesh of the birds and discarded the remainder when their dads were looking the other way. Dad and Sam often reminisced about the way they would snare rabbits and woodchucks. For rabbits, a bare steel wire would be formed in the shape of a noose and tied to a small tree or large rock adjacent to a rabbit hole. The noose would be placed at just the right circumference and elevation over a hole's exit. Woodchuck snares were less humane. Large fishhooks would be attached to a stick and rammed repeatedly into the woodchuck's lair. After some prodding, the angry critter would snap at the probe, which led to its downfall. The animal steadfastly wedged its four legs to the walls of the tunnel and could not be dislodged until becoming weakened under the sustained pressure from the boys, who often took their turn when the other became fatigued. When not in the mine, Nonno did his best to bring wild game and fresh meat to the table. There were also two private reservoirs operated by a major water utility within three or four miles east of Old Boston. These were referred to as "The Small Dam" (Gardner Creek Reservoir) and "The Big Dam" (Mill Creek Reservoir). When Nonno could borrow a stick or two of dynamite from the mine, the reservoirs would yield a few pounds of perch and sunfish.

The shack that Nonna inherited from her first husband was truly dilapidated. Nonna and Nonno did their best to seal out the frigid winter weather common to Northeastern Pennsylvania, until Nonna came up with the ultimate solution. It is a bit of a mystery to understand how they could have afforded insurance even for a shanty like this. Perhaps with a loan from Nonna's sister in Plains or her brother in Corklain, which is east of Pittston (near top of figure 1), they were able to purchase home insurance. One day, while Nonno was at work, Dad, who was just a young boy at the time, began running toward the home and yelling (but in Italian), "Momma, the house is on fire!" Dad recounted that Nonna was standing nearby and casually responded (in Italian), "Be quiet and go play!" The new home built with the help of the insurance company after the "cooking accident" was a modest two-story wood-framed house built adjacent to the remains of the previous shack. After a number of renovations by recent owners, it still stands today. Nonna used the remaining foundation of the nearby burned-out structure as an oven and safe location for baking home-made bread. Remarkably, when I inserted Old Boston Road, Pennsylvania, in Google Earth in early 2014, the program's pointer settled on this site.

Sometime around 1925 or 1926, Uncle Ted began working for a kind gentleman who owned an auto sales and repair shop on South Main Street, Pittston. The gentleman's name was Mike Barber, who, many years later moved his business, Barber Motors, across the Susquehanna River to West Pittston (upper left corner of figure 1). During such hard times, Uncle Ted's pay was as little as $1 per day; however, he rose to a position of responsibility in the company and persuaded Mr. Barber to let his stepbrothers—Uncle Army, Uncle Nello, and Dad—work at the garage after each graduated (1935–1938) from Jenkins Township High School in Sebastapool. In a large photo taken of Dad's 1937 high school graduation class, he appears standing in the top row on the school's front steps with one hand on hip and chin slightly raised. By the proud pose and expression on his face and knowing how he labored in the years that followed, I am quite certain I know precisely what was going through his mind at the moment the photo was snapped. Although no one smiled much in photos taken during that period, his particularly determined pose and expression says, "I will succeed!" Typically, the boys agreed to work at Barber Motors for five or six months without pay until they learned a trade, then they could begin receiving a weekly pay of a few dollars. Even though hardship continued, the family seemed to enter a new era of modest sustainability. On Saturday evening, even a dime might now be available to view the weekly movie projected on a small screen on the second floor of the Old Boston Club House.

Dad and Mother met at a dance at the Fire Hose House on Main Street, Dupont (Upper right corner of Figure 1) in 1939, across from 323 Main Street where Mother lived with her parents, three sisters, and four brothers. The music of Tommy Dorsey and Glen Miller is nostalgic for me today, even though its era of prominence existed before I was old enough to remember it.

Before their marriage, Mother wrote in her diary that when returning to Dupont on a bus from Pittston one day, one boyfriend was waiting at the first bus stop on Main Street, while Dad was a little further east at the second stop. She wrote that at the spur of the moment, she decided to tell the driver that she was getting off at the second stop. I joked (poorly) with her many years later, "Whew, that was a close call. I nearly didn't make it!" Nevertheless, if I knew the driver's name, I would send him a bottle of Schenley every Christmas. Dad and Mother married in 1940 and moved in with Nonna and Nonno at the old homestead in Old Boston. One or two years later, they rented an apartment in a house on the west side of Old Boston where we lived for two more years. With the help of Google Earth, I confirmed recently, from a distance of 2,200 miles, that the small house still stands today on the east side of the road. It is a sagging, abandoned, deteriorated structure of which I (again poorly) joke, "Is in the same condition I created and left it sixty-eight years ago."

CHAPTER IV

DETERMINATION (1940-1950)

I was born in 1942, and around the same time, Dad became an anthracite miner despite Nonno's efforts to keep all of his sons out of the mines. According to Uncle Gildo, one miner at the Old Boston Club House bragged to Nonno about the few dollars his son made weekly at the local colliery and sarcastically asked Nonno, "How much do your boys make in the auto shop?" The miner knew Dad and his brothers made nothing as they worked hard to learn a trade. Nonno replied, "I don't care how much money your son makes at the colliery. I don't want my boys in the mines!" One evening, about one year after Nonno had passed away, Dad returned home from the auto shop and found his younger brother picking at a small coal outcrop about 250 feet east of the house. Uncle Gildo had found the seam and was taking the coal to Nonna's stove and baking oven. In the days that followed, Dad continued to hand-dig the small outcrop each evening after work at the auto shop until he decided to quit the shop and devote all of his effort to the small Old Boston Mine (Location H in figure 1).

With the same creativity and energy he displayed throughout his life, Dad either purchased or rented an old Ford Model A or T, removed the wheels, and rigged the rear axle with a cable drum to pull a small coal car out of the mine. He built a wood chute at the mouth of the mine so that the coal car could be dumped into a truck. He hand-dug a sloping ramp so that the truck could be backed down under the chute. A friend from Old Boston, Gino, had a small dump truck and became Dad's partner in the doghole. It is unknown if they mined the coal legally by paying a royalty to the large coal company that owned the mining rights or if they mined the coal without the knowledge of the coal company. Such small mining operations without the knowledge of the coal's rightful owners were referred to as bootlegging. I suspect that soon, the owner found out and demanded royalty or lease payments. Such payment was usually around 10 percent of the value of the sale at the breaker where the coal was crushed, screened, washed, and sorted for retail sales to homes and industry. A picture of an anthracite breaker similar to the hundreds that once dotted Northeastern Pennsylvania is shown in figure 2.

Mother recalls that even as a tot only two or three years old, I took substantial interest in the mine's progress. When Dad descended the cellar stairs each evening to remove his dirty mining clothes and clean up, Mother recalls that I would call out down the stairs, "Pete, how many cars of coal today? Pete, how many loads did Gino make with the truck?" Of course, I can't recall the exact questions or response, but it probably didn't earn Dad and Gino more than a few dollars each after they purchased supplies and paid the two or three men on their payroll. Dad once recounted how he would enter the mine around 5:00 each morning and make many trips in and out, carrying two buckets to remove accumulated groundwater so that miners arriving at 7:00 a.m. would be able to work in a reasonably dry mine chamber.

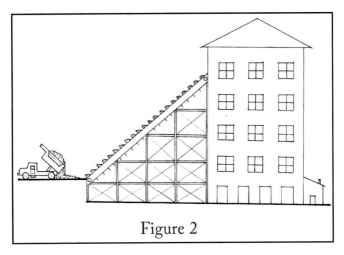

Figure 2

Nevertheless, it wouldn't be long before Dad could replace the makeshift Ford Hoist with a real mine hoist and purchase a small water pump. Even after Dad had his first serious mine accident around 1943—a broken leg—he was undeterred. After hobbling on crutches for several weeks, Dad started a new doghole about one-quarter mile south of the initial one, in a desolate area outside Old Boston known as Pickaway. He and Gino built a wood tipple, installed a used mine hoist in a shanty, and hoisted the coal cars up a steep slope to the tipple, which could hold forty or fifty tons. (See figure 3 for a typical coal tipple.) Pickaway is now occupied by a very large manufacturing plant.

Around 1947, I began to have occasional opportunities to see the mine. Dad had asked his brother, Elmo, to leave high school at Jenkins Township in the tenth grade and begin hauling the coal to the breaker with the small dump truck that Dad and Gino owned. Dad later expressed regret at taking his kid brother out of school, but I am certain that he did so to improve the economic welfare of his mother, brother, and sister who still lived in Old Boston. By this time, Dad and Mother had moved out of Old Boston and rented an apartment on Ziegler Street in Dupont, around the corner from where Mother's parents lived on Main Street. I can't recall my childhood toys, but I can recall my excitement whenever Uncle Elmo would pick me up at our home in Dupont and take me with him to load the truck at the tipple and haul the coal to the breaker. In 1947, Dad and Gino bought a big green Brockway dump truck similar to the one shown in figure 4. At age seventeen or eighteen, Uncle Elmo artistically painted the underside frame, wheel hubs, and front grille a bright yellow, built up the truck's steel box with wood sideboards so it could carry a maximum load, and blasted the air horn at every slow driver in front of him. With the built-up sideboards, the heavy Brockway with a load of coal was usually over the legal weight limit for a single-axle Z-license truck, which had a legal capacity of around eleven tons, but my uncle always heaped the truck as much as possible. State police patrolled the highways with portable scales; however, my uncle did not seem to care and was constantly ticketed. The penalty was usually a cash fine or a night in jail, and to my best knowledge, Uncle Elmo never paid any fines. I often asked my parents to allow me to spend some evenings with my uncle and Nonna in Old Boston so I could enjoy the excitement of riding the truck between the mine and breaker the next day. During one visit, Nonna intentionally gave me too much homemade wine, and even though I cried with dizziness, I can still recall the mischievous grin on her face as she sent me to sleep after her prank. Eventually, I concluded that this was an example of where Dad got his penchant for practical jokes, but more about that later.

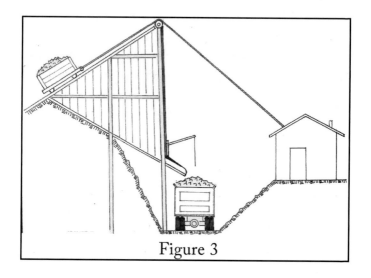

Figure 3

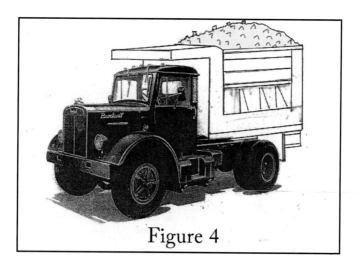

Figure 4

One day, the Brockway was stopped near the top of a snowy hill on the dirt road leading to the mine, and I got out of the truck to watch my uncle shovel ashes in front of the rear tires. Suddenly, the hand brake accidentally disengaged and the truck sped down the steep hill backward. Uncle Elmo ran like a deer to catch up to it, jumped behind the wheel, and guided it safely as it sped backward around a sharp curve at the bottom of the hill. I often wondered if my uncle intentionally steered the truck to the edge of deep strip mine pits to give me a thrill. At one such pit, the fully loaded truck had to make a sharp 90-degree turn to the right around a deep strip mine at about five or ten miles an hour. There was also a depression on the right side of the rocky road so that the top-heavy truck tipped precariously to the right as we rounded the curve. I looked down through the window at the deep pit three or four feet to my right and quickly glanced a startled look back toward my uncle on my left side. I can recall that by the expression on his face, he suddenly felt uncomfortable with his planned, or unplanned, thrill. Fortunately, the truck gradually leveled off as we continued slowly through the depression and around the curve. When we returned later for the next load, Dad obviously wasn't thrilled, either by what he had seen and had already placed a large slab of rock in the depression to force the truck further from the edge of the pit on subsequent loads.

When riding with my uncle, however, my biggest challenge was not in enduring his fabricated thrills, but to ignore the seminude photos of Marilyn Monroe that he had taped overhead across the ceiling of the truck's cab. Also difficult to ignore was the colorful rendering of a little puppy pulling at the hem of a leggy model's negligee as she reached out her doorway to pick up a newspaper on her front porch. After touring the Sistine Chapel at the Vatican in Rome forty years later, I joked (not so poorly) to a puzzled tour guide that Michelangelo's art on the ceiling reminded me of my uncle's dump truck.

I also began to meet Dad's partner, Gino, frequently and came to admire the husky brute greatly. When I was a boy, he seemed hard and unapproachable. When I was six or seven, I was riding with him when he entered a gas station and handed me an ice cream treat when he retuned to the pickup. I politely said, "Wow, thank you!" Without turning his head, which seemed unsupported by a neck, and out of the corner of his eye and side of his mouth, with a very sarcastic grin, he muttered, "Cut the crap, kid!" As time passed, I gradually realized it was all part of his John Wayne imitation, and he was hiding a heart of gold.

When I was between the ages of five and eight, Dad began to take me along to the mine more and more. Dad's version of take-your-child-to-work day occurred every week or two, and I suspect it was mostly for my own amusement. It's also possible he sensed that I was intensely interested. One day at about 1:00 a.m., he and Uncle Elmo attached a cable to a large wood shanty on wood skids at an abandoned mine in Laflin (bottom of figure 1), and I watched my uncle tow it behind the dump truck down Highway 315 to Old Boston. A little old retired miner by the name of Tucci (pronounced Tuuchee) rented the shanty from Nonna and also paid her for cooked meals and homemade wine. Nonna also catered homemade dinners and wine for other immigrant miners who lived in nearby shanties, such as Jack the Spaniard, and others whose names are more difficult to recall. During the Depression, Nonna's basement had been a popular speakeasy for miners in the Settlement.

Tucci often spoke with pride of his World War I service under General Black Jack Pershing, but turned comic whenever Nonna requested payment after a few glasses of vino. With a toothless smile and face flushed red as the wine he drank, the frail little man typically responded, "Try get!" It was also comical to watch the two drinking wine on Nonna's porch, snacking garden-grown garlic, and arguing very animatedly about the destination city of overhead planes departing from the airport in Avoca. I sometimes wonder how many immigrant miners ended up like Tucci after being led to America and a path of extreme hardship by exaggerated ads for miners circulated in Europe. Initially, there was the WOP (Without Official Papers) tag on his lapel that also noted his destination, so the agent at Ellis Island could lead Tucci to the proper bus or train. Then he was led into a dangerous mine where he would battle to survive and make one or two dollars each day. Later, his adopted country would lead him to a war in Europe, where he continued to battle to survive. Subsequently, he returned to dangerous mines and, later, battled to breathe through black lungs lacerated by coal dust.

Finally, and at a relatively early age, his decimated body would be lead to a cemetery in Dupont, where no one knows he ever existed. I suspect there were many other Tuccis who were led down similar sad paths in the anthracite coalfields.

Other than occasionally running to fetch a shovel or tool for Dad, I certainly could not contribute much and never entered the mines in those very early years before 1950. On countless occasions, I would be left in the pickup while he crawled into some old abandoned, partially collapsed mine in search of coal. Dad did not have any political affiliations to give him mining opportunities. He searched underground alone and relentlessly to find them. I sat for hours alone in the pickup, hopeful that he would reemerge soon and safely. When I was eight years old, it became apparent Dad wanted me to learn to work. In 1950, he decided to build a restaurant, with a new home above it, on the east side of Highway 315, one mile south of Dupont (Location J in figure 1). He would work in the mine during the day and on the construction of the restaurant and home in the evening. He set up a portable concrete mixer and loaded it with cement, sand, stone, and water. At age eight, there wasn't much I could do to assist with this hard labor; but once he tilted the mixer and deposited the concrete on the ground, he needed me to hold one end of the screed board that he and I moved along the top of the fresh concrete to level it. Although he had hired a carpenter, Ceilio, to work on the home during the day, Dad cut and nailed wood studs, joists, and plywood flooring each evening. I helped a little by holding the lumber as he cut and nailed it. On one occasion, he had a spotlight positioned so we could work into the evening. Uncle Mike visited the site with a carload of his little nieces and nephews and was taking them to an outdoor movie (Comerford Drive-In Theater) that had just been built across the highway from our new restaurant and home. He asked Dad if I could join them, and Dad politely said, "No, I need him." I do not recall feeling any disappointment and, at the time, quite likely appreciated the subtle hint of my manhood in the presence of my uppity little sister, Carol, and usually indifferent smaller cousins.

During the following Christmas or the next, I told Mother that I would like to give Dad a black lunch bucket and coffee thermos as a gift. I had noticed that almost all miners carried their lunch in black lunch buckets, but Dad carried his in a brown paper bag. I felt terrific after Dad opened his gift, but he probably felt the pail shaped like a mail box with leather handle was too conventional. Besides, he rarely took the time to eat lunch, anyway, while loading coal. I saw him later that evening take a steel nail and inscribe my own name in the enamel coating on the inside. It was then that I first suspected his plan for my education in Anthracite Grade School and the meaning of the writing on the wall of the lunch bucket.

CHAPTER V

FIRST DAY OF ANTHRACITE GRADE SCHOOL (1951)

By this point in time, Dad had decided that the quickest way to mine coal near the outcrop was to uncover the vein with the bulldozer, excavate a hole to store eighty to hundred tons at the mouth of the mine, and have Uncle Elmo load the coal on the Brockway with a steam shovel. A picture of a steam shovel similar to Dad's is shown in figure 5. Just as Uncle Elmo built up the box of the Brockway to haul a maximum load, Dad welded steel plates to the bucket of the steam shovel so it could lift one ton of coal instead of three-fourths of a ton. Maximum production was essential in every phase of their work. Uncle Mike often coached me to play baseball with what he called Jinnegar. The web defines it as a now outdated term ball players used prior to World War II to describe how the game should be played with energy, focus, and intensity. Dad, Gino, and Uncle Elmo mined and loaded anthracite with tons of jinnegar. Even when I see a dump truck without side boards today, I humorously conclude, "There goes a guy without jinnegar or passion!"

The coal was dragged out of the mine by a lever-operated mechanical loader (figure 6) that pulled a bucket or scoop with a coal capacity of about one ton (figure 7). Again, with a certain creative genius, Dad had a welder fabricate the bucket so that it was lightweight and could be lifted by a single miner and strategically placed behind a pile of coal. The frame was made of tubing instead of solid steel bars. The bottom of the vertical side plate was curved inward all around so that it could scoop the coal. Similar equipment exists at the Anthracite Museum in Scranton, but in comparison, the museum equipment is heavy, awkward, and certainly not as efficient. The mechanical loader was about the size of a large kitchen table. One part contained a 30 horsepower electric motor if electricity existed at the mine or a gasoline engine if no electricity existed. The second component contained two cable drums, each operated by depressing a steel lever at the top of each drum. When the right lever was depressed, the right drum reeled in the main three-fourth inch steel cable that dragged the loaded scoop out of the mine. By pressing down hard on the lever, the cable and scoop traveled faster. When the left lever was depressed, the left drum reeled in a 1/2" cable tail rope that ran from the drum back into the mine, around a steel pulley at the face where the men were working, and back out to the rear of the scoop so it could be dragged back to the miners. The main and tail rope cables can be seen in figures 6 and 7. A doghole might function for seven or nine months because the mechanical loader only had a horizontal mining range of 700 or 800 feet. Then the equipment was moved a few hundred feet to a new doghole, or Dad might discover a more profitable mining opportunity a few miles away.

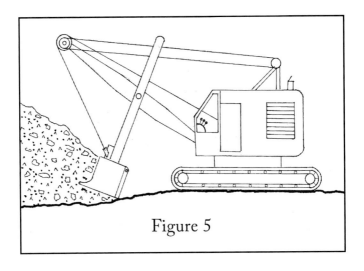

Figure 5

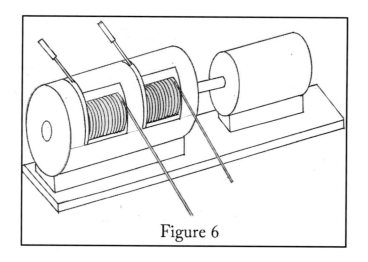

Figure 6

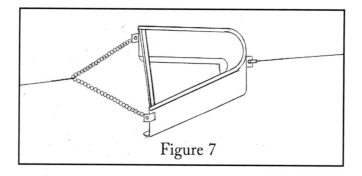

Figure 7

From the winter of 1951 to the spring of 1959, I usually was behind the mechanical loader when I was not in school, and my initial anthracite school class occurred during my Christmas vacation in the fifth grade. I rode with Dad to his mine in Irish Hill, (location K in figure 1) east of Old Boston, which we accessed by driving the two-lane paved road east from Dupont through Suscon (right side of fig. 1) and then traveled about two miles south on a dirt road owned and operated by a dynamite (powder) sales company. Irish Hill is now mostly covered by industrial warehouses and tractor-trailer terminals, but in 1951, the powder company made and stored dynamite in several steel buildings along the dirt road. The company allowed Dad to use the very private road because he agreed to help them grade and maintain the road with his bulldozer. The winter weather was bitter and the mechanical loader was in a 15' × 15' × 8' high wood shanty that had a small coal stove in one corner. Heavy winds from the west wracked the shanty and hillside, as they do today on eleven or twelve huge wind turbines that now line the top of nearby Bald Mountain, slightly east of Irish Hill.

Dad explained to me that when he touched two wires together three times inside the mine, the bell in the shanty would ring three times and it meant I had to depress the lever on the tail rope drum to pull the bucket back into the mine. He started to say, "And when you hear one bell—", at which time I interrupted him and said, "I know. It means I stop the bucket." Dad and his friend, Sam, laughed and Sam said, "He already knows!" Of course, I had watched other operators, and the signaling system was, in fact, very simple. From a stopped position, a single bell meant to pull the bucket (or scoop) forward very slowly because a miner was kneeling on top of the scoop, using his weight to press the scoop into the side of the coal pile. Two bells meant the miner was off the bucket, the bucket was full, and it should be pulled out of the mine at full speed. Twenty bells meant the miners wanted me to coil the main cable in front of the scoop around a group of wood props and drag the props back into the mine so they could measure, cut, and prop the roof where the previous cut of coal had been removed. Ten slow rings was the signal that the bell should be disconnected and wires reconnected to an electric switchbox in the shanty. Then the miners could use the electric drill to auger holes to insert sticks of dynamite for the next cut of coal.

After my initial shanty classroom training, Dad, Sam, and one other miner entered the doghole, and I could hear them as they shuffled along 100 to 150 feet into the mine. Dad was probably assuring the miners that I knew what to do. Suddenly, I heard a distant loud thud, after which I could hear the three miners running back out toward the mine entrance. They were relieved to see that I was standing calmly at the shanty door and had not tossed gasoline from a nearby can onto the dormant stove fire. The thud we all heard was the ominous sound of a roof collapse in an abandoned mine chamber that interconnected nearby with our doghole.

My biggest concern at that mine was not the heavy winds and sub-freezing temperatures, running the loader, or manipulation of electrical switchboxes. *It was bears!* We were in a remote wooded area, two to three miles from the nearest homes, and I had heard many stories about bear hunting in that region. There was an axe in the shanty, and I always made sure it was within arm's reach. One day, I was entirely certain I saw a bear track in the snow just behind the shanty, and I refused to respond to the bell signals from the miners. Dad came out and asked, "What's wrong?" In terror, I pointed and said, "There's a bear track!" He laughed and said it was just the sunlight reflecting off the windowpane and melting the snow in spots. Nevertheless, I always kept the axe nearby, and in the summer, it also lessened my fear of rattlers and copperheads that I had heard slither among the nearby rock ledges.

About 600 feet from this mine, there was a large pipeline that the local water company used to augment the storage at the reservoir behind the small dam. One day during the summer, the miners asked me to go to the pipeline and fill a few water bottles in an opening at the top of the pipe. While filling the bottles, the brush behind me began to rustle, and I heard a distinct growl. I immediately took off running in the opposite direction and down the dirt road nearby that was the access to the mine, throwing the water bottles aside along the way. As I approached the miners, Dad asked (again), "What's wrong?" Terrified, I responded, "There's a bear chasing me!" The miners laughed, and I learned later that Sam had sent another miner to act out the role of the bear. Many years later, whenever I would visit Sam at his home in Browntown, he would retell the story with some embellishments, suggesting I had also lost my shoes while running frantically from the bear that I only thought was chasing me.

Louis Ronald Scatena

Dad never lost his family's depression era need to hunt and put fresh meat on the dinner table, and it did not matter if the game was in hunting season. He usually carried a vintage 12-gage Fox double-barrel shotgun behind the seat of the pickup and would quickly jamb the brakes whenever any unlucky critter crossed the dirt road leading to the mine. On one occasion, his target was a flock of a dozen or more pigeons and I recall one of the wounded birds diving beak first, smashing kamikaze style into the side of the pickup near where I was standing. I obviously picked up on the habit of nabbing critters, and one day while riding with another miner, I asked him to stop when a woodchuck crossed the dirt road. I stoned the animal and placed his carcass in our basement until such time that I could skin him and clean the meat. An hour later, I heard Mother shriek as the varmint scampered around our basement.

Occasionally after work, and before I was old enough to carry a hunting rifle, Dad and I would walk into the hills near the mine on Irish Hill in search of deer. He would wave his arms and point in the direction he wanted me to circle through the woods to flush any deer to the point where he would be posted. For example, he might say, "Walk down this trail for 5 minutes, or about 1,000 feet, until you come to another trail off to the left. Take that for about 5 minutes, then turn left and come back up the hill, and I (pointing) will be standing on that rock ledge over there." Of course, it all seemed very clear until I started wandering, confused, back up the hill through the thick woods and swamps. On that day, however, I heard the old Fox shotgun ring out,

Dad came over to where he spotted me walking, and I followed him up the hill to the kill. He steadied the deer on his left shoulder with his left arm and carried the gun in his right hand, as I walked along behind him down to the pickup. Most boys thought their Dad was superman, but I was different—I *knew* Dad was Superman! I also recall feeling quite content with my part in the team effort. A few years later, after I became old enough for a hunting license, my teamwork during a similar deer flush did not go so well. I wandered through an opening in a fence line in Suscon and found myself standing in the center of a complex of dynamite storage buildings with my new 16-gage shotgun. Workers yelled as I scurried back through the opening. Their nervousness was quite understandable since one or two of their co-workers from Dupont had been killed in an accidental explosion there only a few months earlier.

Dad's Fox shotgun had an interesting history. Sometime during the depression, a series of well-publicized crimes were committed in Old Boston and the weapon was never recovered before or during the trial of the accused. As a young boy, Dad had come across the hiding place where the accused had stashed the weapon to avoid incrimination. Nonno hunted with the gun for years afterward, and Nonna passed it on to Dad after Nonno died.

Besides deer hunting, Dad had a passion for accordion music, but when he was a boy, buying an accordion and taking lessons was out of the question during the depression. One evening in 1951, he walked into our home playing a semi-recognizable tune, probably his favorite, "Mona Lisa," on a used accordion he had purchased. He announced, "You're going to start taking lessons and you'll be the best around!" Dad was bewildered when I responded tearfully, and Mother had to explain to him, "He's afraid of disappointing you." It was not easy to avoid disappointing Dad. He wanted me to excel at everything. When I was nine, he visited one of my little league games in Dupont just in time to see me strike out in the bottom of the ninth inning to lose the game for my team. On the way home, I shrunk down in the seat as, looking out of the corner of his eye, he admonished, "You had to strike out?" There has been a similar situation commercialized on TV recently where the father consoles the boy on the way home. Dad would not have been ideal for that commercial. Now that I think of it, I, too, would have failed the screen test for the role of the father many years later after watching my own son's initial Pop Warner football games. To other fathers standing next to me on the sidelines, I may have appeared uninvolved, but fidgety. In reality, hands on hips, folded arms, or hand through hair were well-rehearsed signals that told Pete precisely how I wanted him to fire off the defensive line. To confirm he was not just looking in my direction to humor me, I also required that he acknowledge receipt and understanding of each signal by glancing in my direction while he pretended to adjust his facemask. Parents and coaches were always puzzled when he sometimes threw the opposing quarterback to the ground before the ball was hiked.

Two or three years after my ninth-inning strike-out, Dad enjoyed taking other miners to my little league games to watch me play when I was older and more skillful. I also learned to play the accordion decently, mostly because Dad sternly directed me to practice each evening. A few years later at the Cetta Parrish music store on the square in Scranton, my accordion teacher, Arnold, who was originally from New Boston (figure 1) and a longtime friend of the family, winced at the sight of my keyboard hands and fingernails, which were encrusted with hard-to-remove anthracite grime. He closed his office door after I stepped out, and from a distance through the glass wall of his office, I could see the frail little music teacher looking up at Dad and taking him to task about my labor at the mine. Dad listened politely and Arnold soon realized it was like water off a duck's back. Little did Arnold know that like Dad, I was indifferent to the work.

To the best of my knowledge, my performance on the mechanical loader in my first year was satisfactory, as it would be for the next seven years. On one or two occasions, Sam told Dad that I did not operate the loader very well when Dad was not in the mine and that I operated it much better when Dad was there. He was probably right and fortunate that Dad was almost always there. On those rare occasions that he was unhappy with my performance, Sam would give me a blast of very rapid 30+ bell rings to let me know he was perturbed. I think it was mostly his way of getting my goat, as he always seemed to enjoy doing, even when we hunted together a few years later. After I shot a deer, Sam would say, "You should have shot two." At my little league games, Sam would say, "G'wan, you're too big to play with those kids." Sam was best man at Mother and Dad's wedding and my life-long personal friend until he passed away in 2011 at age ninety-three.

CHAPTER VI

IRISH HILL (1952)

The miners from Old Boston had names for all of the hills and valleys east of the settlement, names like Irish Hill, Dunney's, Pinchko's, Jumper's, etc. At the mine in Irish Hill, coal production and Dad's good fortune began to escalate, and Dad decided to start a second mine nearby. Not only was the vein higher than any Dad mined previously, but it was flat, well defined, and only overlain by twenty-five to thirty feet of a good, solid roof rock. By drilling and blasting the rock and excavating a large pit with the bulldozer, the coal seam could be quickly exposed. Dad and Gino had purchased a brand new D-7 Caterpillar with the help of insurance money after their little World War II surplus A-C International dozer toppled approximately eighty feet into a deep strip mine. The old dozer had a bad habit of jumping out of gear and that likely led to the accident.

At the Irish Hill mine, I helped Dad build a wood ramp up and out of the mine to the storage pit. (See figure 8 for the Irish Hill Mine Ramp.) I scampered up and down the ramp, fetching tools and holding planks as he cut and nailed them. When finished, the scoop ran up and down the ramp smoothly, and I felt good about my small role in its construction. Once set up, the mechanical loader with three miners underground could produce 80 to 100 tons each day. Dad and Gino received about $5 to $5.50 per ton from the breaker. Miners made $12 to $14 per day, the owner of the coal rights was paid about 50 cents per ton, and Uncle Elmo received 50 to 60 cents per ton to load and haul the coal to the breaker. By this time, Uncle Elmo had married Aunt Jean and the tribute to Marilyn Monroe on the "Sistine Ceiling" of the Brockway had been removed. Dad began paying me $5 per day, and I still recall my first check for $60 for two weeks' work. Each summer, I received a $1 per day pay increase and enjoyed checking the growing balance in my bankbook every two weeks after Mother deposited my paycheck. From my perspective, life was good. I was being paid to do exciting work with my dad!

Occasionally at the end of a day's work, Dad and the other miners would meet in the basement under our restaurant and drink quarts of cold beer, which would be deducted from the miners' pay. I, also, would select from a case of soda that contained multiple flavored bottles, and Dad directed Mother to deduct the case of soda from my pay. Reflecting back on that incident, I realize now that I probably should have filed a labor grievance, especially since I was already mowing grass, washing the car, and daily tending to our home's coal stove and ashes without a weekly allowance! Of course, I joke badly (again) and cannot recall ever complaining to Dad about anything.

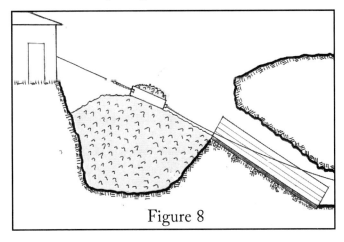

Figure 8

One could argue, however, that in teaching his lesson, Dad may have occasionally been overly exuberant. In looking back, I have fond memories of that black-faced, grimy group sitting on the concrete floor with their backs against the foundation wall near the coal bin, laughing, joking, and washing the coal dust from their throats. Many years later, one miner, Ernie, asked me if I remembered the small bolt of lightning that penetrated a basement window near where we were sprawled during a rainstorm outside. He maintained he saw the lightning strike me, but I concluded his vision of the event was distorted by the cold beer.

To add to Dad's good fortunes, the owner of the coal rights asked a nearby competitor to terminate their operation because the competitor's production was unsatisfactory. The competitor had built a tipple, installed a hoist, and a gangway with a set of rails to the tipple. A gangway is a main tunnel about eight feet wide by eight feet high. The top half of the gangway is cut through coal, but the bottom half is painstakingly cut through solid rock to provide enough height to run coal cars on a rail track. Their operation used shakers to bring coal out of the side chambers and drop it into the parked coal cars in the gangway. Shakers were 18" wide steel chutes that sat a foot or two above the floor of the vein. The long chute was supported on electrically operated, vertical rocker arms that were spaced every 10 to 15 feet along the length of the chute. The chute constantly rocked back and forward, sliding the coal out to the mine car with each sudden, forward thrust. Shakers were an old mining system that was falling into disuse at that time because almost every pound of coal had to be hand-shoveled onto the chute. With the mechanical loader , however, the miner only had to position the scoop behind or on the side of a pile of coal, and one ton was quickly on its way to the pit outside. Gangway, hoist, and tipple made sense when the vein was very deep and/or the mining was occurring beneath a town or developed region. In remote areas, however, Dad knew that conventional gangway, hoist, and tipple did not make economic sense where shallow veins could easily, and quickly, be revealed with a bulldozer to set up access tunnels. Dad also concluded that underground mining made more sense economically than strip-mining the solid rock. In strip-mining, and in addition to lease payments to the owner of the rights to the coal, the operator also had to pay the owner of the land a performance bond of several thousand dollars. The mine operator would receive the bond back only if he restored the ground surface to its original condition after the strip-mining was complete.

Running the mechanical loader was a messy job. The internal drive shaft of the loader had to be lubricated periodically and after a few hours of heated operation, the drive shaft bearings began to spit hot grease at the operator. Most loader operators cut and clamped cardboard to the drums to intercept the mess and faced with the task of washing my clothes, Mother probably wished I took time to do the same. As the steel cables in the drum became worn, they also began gradually shredding and spewing tiny steel fragments. Cardboard would have also helped to block the fragments. Almost all coal veins contain one or two thin embedded seams of slate rock, which miners called boney. As Uncle Elmo loaded each truckload, it was my job to turn off the mechanical loader, jump into the box of the truck, and pitch out the boney as he dumped each bucket into the truck with the steam shovel. If a slab of rock was too heavy for me, my uncle would jump up into the box of the truck and toss it out. No slab was too large for him. Often, the switch that he pressed to release the coal from the bucket of the old steam shovel didn't function and I had to yank on the small cable that opened the trap door at the bottom of the bucket. My uncle worked with jinnegar, loading and turning the steam shovel rapidly, jogging to the cab of the truck, and speeding to the breaker seven to eight miles away in Moosic, Old Forge, or Hughestown (near top of figure 1).

At the breaker, the weighmaster would read the scale in pounds and give my uncle a receipt for the weight of the coal. From his elevated position in the scale house, the weighmaster could easily assess the quality of the coal on top of the truck and dock the scale's measured weight by a few hundred or more pounds, if he did not like what he saw. For this reason, it was not only necessary for me to remove boney from the truck, but also place the best coal chunks at the front of the box, or temporarily on the canopy over the truck's cab so they could be later distributed to dress up the top when the truck was full. The chunks were like the icing on the cake. In this manner, not only did the coal on top of the truck look good to the weighmaster, but chunks placed at the front of the box also appeared at the top of the pile when the load was dumped into the breaker's hopper. It paid to be nice to the weighmaster and Dad and Uncle Elmo saw to it that the weighmaster received a bottle of Schenley or Old Overholt periodically.

One day, an unhappy weighmaster told my uncle and another trucker that there was a lot of boney showing up on the conveyor to the top of the breaker, and he instructed both drivers to dump their loads on the ground near the hopper for closer inspection. The other driver poked at his load with a shovel, proclaiming the load was in order. Uncle Elmo grabbed the shovel from his hands and dug down two or three feet through the icing to expose all the boney and undesirable material.

On some rare occasions when coal was in very great demand, however, the weighmaster's interest in quality waned and my uncle said it was not necessary to remove the boney. With the steam shovel, he would even load a few buckets of rock from the side of the storage pit, hiding it inside the truck box against the tailgate. By the end of the life of a doghole, the storage pit had usually grown to double its original size. This may appear dishonest, but I prefer to call it, "bending the truth." At that time, men continuing to emerge from the dark shadows of the Great Depression bent it a lot.

CHAPTER VII

UNDERGROUND (1953)

Rarely did Dad instruct me to enter dogholes, but for a few days that summer, he asked me to join him at the mine face after I had pulled that day's cut of coal to the pit with the loader. In later years, I concluded that he felt this was a necessary chapter in my education and also felt this particular doghole at Irish Hill was relatively safe. In looking back, I can say it certainly was not even remotely as treacherous as the other seven or eight dogholes that I can recall. On this day, Dad said that I should put on a helmet and lamp and follow the tail rope back to the mine face where I would help him set props and drill the holes for the next cut of coal. This was typically done near the end of the shift so that gases from the detonation would eventually subside that evening before the miners returned to the mine the next morning. The helmet was still a little loose over my baseball cap, and with boots and elevated helmet, I could stand erect in the five-foot high mine, with an inch or two to spare.

As I followed the tail rope back to the miners, I reached an area where the roof and floor pinched close together to allow a crawl space of only about fourteen or fifteen inches. I was apprehensive about wiggling through the space and noticed that at some distance to the left and right, the vein seemed to be higher. However, I was afraid of inadvertently wandering off into the seemingly endless maze of chambers and elected to pass through the tight space instead. Years later, I was doubtful when a retired miner told me he once worked in a low vein for days without being able to roll on his side or back throughout a work shift. Then I recalled my own experience wiggling under the low roof, and it dawned on me that what the old miner told me was quite probable. In recent years, when my wife asks me if I had a "difficult day at the office," I think of my dad and other miners drilling, shoveling, and setting props in a pinched vein.

On the day of my first trip underground, I mostly walked erect for 6 or 700 feet and soon reached the mine face where I began to help Dad cut and set props. With an ax, he would cut a small hitch (or depression) in the rock floor of the mine that was a little larger than the nine- or ten-inch diameter of the prop. He measured the distance from the bottom of the hitch to the roof allowing an inch or two for the wedge-shaped wood cap pieces that he would sledge hammer into place to wedge the prop to the roof. For a typical view of mine props with cap pieces and hitches, see figure 12. (See

Index at back for location of all figures.) It took several minutes of experience with the large, very sharp, two-man saw before I learned to pull horizontally without any vertical weight on the handle so the saw would not bind. I do not know why a power saw wasn't used, but perhaps, it was prohibited by mine safety regulations at that time.

Normally, it took two men to push the electric drill into the coal horizontally to create the eight or nine foot long drill hole. See figure 9 for three types of mining drills, including an electric drill in the center. After several holes, the carbide drill bit attached at the end of the drill became worn, and no amount of force could advance the drill through the anthracite. The worn bits were replaced periodically, and Dad resharpened them each evening on a grinding wheel in the basement of our home. A row of ten or twelve holes, each two or three feet apart, were drilled just above the floor of the vein, and another similar row just below the roof. When the miners were standing and leaning forward on the drill, they could spread their feet so they had sufficient leverage to force the drill forward. However, the bottom row of drill holes was more difficult to drill because the miners had to push from a kneeling position. Since the nearest line of props was several feet from the face of the pillar, they also could not brace themselves against the props. At times, Dad directed me to sit on the floor with my feet braced to a prop. Then he could sit with his back to my own and push on the drill with his feet while another miner operated the switch on the drill's handle. What I would pay for that photo! When I was not helping with the drill or cutting props, I would fill "tamping bags" with the coarse coal dust that the drill's auger piled outside each drill hole. The filled bags were the same diameter as the drill hole and after three or four sticks of dynamite were pushed into each hole, the tamping bags were rammed into the hole with a wood "tamping stick." When the dynamite was detonated later, the tamping bags forced the blast laterally into the coal seam, instead of back out the drill hole. The first stick of dynamite placed in a drill hole was embedded with a delay fuse attached to a wire that extended to the exterior of the hole. Delays were in time increments of one to ten seconds so that all drill holes did not explode simultaneously and cause a roof collapse.

Miners referred to the practice of angling and spacing drill holes, inserting the right amount of dynamite, and setting the correct delay fuses as cutting coal and considered it an art. When done "artfully" by a skilled miner, the bottom row would be timed to explode first, then the top row to bring the overhanging portion down in chunks. Coal had to be cut properly to prevent excessively small material, which the weighmaster might dock from the real measured weight. Dynamite had to be carefully estimated to prevent the coal from scattering among the props, and drill holes oriented to make the resulting coal pile easily accessible to the scoop. Occasionally after the detonation, a thick seam of coal remained clinging to the roof rock. With a heavy steel bar, the miner would pry the seam of coal down off the roof, and hopefully, without bringing any part of the roof down with it.

After drilling and charging the drill holes was complete, I followed the tail rope back outside to the shanty. Sixty years later, I can still picture the huge grin on Uncle Elmo's face when he saw his blackened, disheveled, half-pint nephew with oversized helmet crawling up the wood ramp.

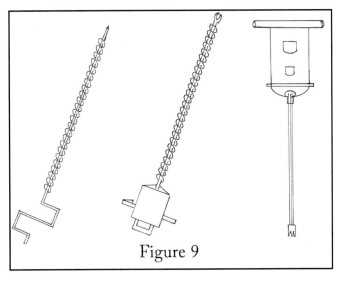

Figure 9

I turned off the power and disconnected the wire to the mine at the fuse box so the miners could connect the wire at their end to the drill holes. After the miners came outside, I reconnected the wire and threw the lever on the fuse box to detonate the drill holes. The ground shook in a series of seven or eight explosions that occurred in one- or two-second intervals.

On one rare occasion, I worked inside the mine while another miner operated the mechanical loader. I sat between two props and touched the ends of the bell wires together whenever Dad said to stop or start the scoop. At one point, Dad and I were shoveling coal side by side and he asked me, "Why did you stop?" I responded that I had a headache, and he said, "Don't you think I have one too!" I know that I could not have been a very productive miner at age eleven, and it is clear to me now that Dad was very focused on my education.

Among the small mining operations during that period, contractual agreements between mine owners were mostly unwritten, and conflicts of interests were common. The legal profession at that time was far less widespread than it is today, now that every small borough seems to have a law office in every shopping plaza. One weekend, we were walking along a remote dirt road near a mine operated by another competitor. The company's equipment was parked nearby and no one was around. Dad began describing to me how I should proceed down the road and swing through the woods to flush any deer out toward where he would be posted with the Fox shotgun. I had proceeded down the road for only a few minutes when I heard a series of six or seven blasts from the shotgun. I ran back as fast as I could to where Dad was standing and saw the windows of the mine equipment were shattered, tires were flat, and water was leaking from the radiators. I looked at Dad and, bewildered, said nothing. With what I distinctly remember as a look of apology, he solemnly said to me, "They owed us $4,000 and refused to pay." For me, the event was remindful of the heroic Don Corleone in the *Godfather*. Sometimes, nasty hits were justified, or so they seemed to the Don and his audience.

On another occasion a few years earlier, Dad sold his bulldozer to another company who discontinued payments after a few months. Dad went to that company's mine early one Sunday morning and drove the dozer down a steep riverbank and, as in old Western movies, continued up the Lackawanna River a substantial distance from that mine to hide the tracks. There, he steered the dozer up the steep bank and loaded it on a truck for the return trip to his mine. A court judge later ruled that the other company had to legally return the dozer to Dad, and Dad had to return the other company's few initial payments. Dad and Gino also experienced material losses at their own mines as well. After a series of such losses, Dad hid at the mine one evening, waiting for the culprits to return. After threatening them with the shotgun, the two intruders took off and never returned. Although the intense strife that existed in the anthracite fields twenty-five or thirty years earlier had dissipated, occasional small vendettas still persisted.

CHAPTER VIII

NEW BOSTON (1954)

Dad had an unusual way of waking me in the morning for work if I lingered in bed. Typically, he would have a shot of whiskey with his morning black coffee, especially during the bitter cold winters common to Northeastern Pennsylvania. He would stir his forefinger in a cup of the concoction near my bed and silently run it along my lips. I could still see that big grin on his face as he retreated through the door, confident that I would be along shortly. The grin always reminded me of Nonna's grin the evening of her prank in Old Boston when she gave me homemade red wine. Often, I would also be a little slow joining Dad in the pickup for the drive to the mine. He typically would begin edging down the driveway, forcing me to run quickly to catch up with him about 100 feet from the house. Dad had a very effective way of communicating with me without saying much. In the same respect, he also did not say much when he made every effort to show me a good time. Examples were the three or four times Dad, Uncle Elmo, Gino, and I made an all-day car trip to see the New York Yankees at Sunday doubleheaders. Prior to one doubleheader, the waitress in the diner across from Yankee Stadium brashly announced, "I guess this is mine," as she pocketed the remaining cash as her tip after Dad paid her for our lunch. She probably knew from experience that she could take advantage of polite coal miners from Scranton, and that they weren't the best tippers in New York. As was his nature, Dad did not raise an objection to her, but the experience was the topic of conversation in the car a number of times during the return trip home. The other primary topic was the amazing speed Mickey Mantle displayed running from first base to home plate, despite failing his army induction physical due to bad knees.

Besides the thrill of Yankee Stadium, there were countless other experiences that Dad shared away from the mine. Examples were the many visits to the Old Boston Italian Citizen's Club, where miners were quick to tell the bartender, "Give the boy a birch beer or candy bar." During bocce matches, the miners were as excited as any National Football League crowd. When a player tossed a bocce thirty-five feet through the air, struck the opposition's bocce to replace it with his own next to the small paulino, the group erupted in a frenzy as if Jim Brown had just dashed for a touchdown. "Costa-Costa!" (Roll it slowly up to the small paulino), "Streesh!" (Roll hard and knock the opponent's bocce out of the way), "Saa'-co-say- ee!"(air strike the opponent's bocce out of the way and replace it near the small paulino for six points), were raucous yells intended to guide the bocce ball. In the game of morra, a group stood in a circle and two opposing players simultaneously yelled their anticipation of the sum of fingers at the instant hands were slammed forward. Yelling their guesses, "Qua'-tro!"(4), "Say–ee!" (6), "Chinq'- que!" (5), etc., as loud as possible seemed part of the game and intended to intimidate their opponent. After an hour, the fatigued group had to retreat to the bar to regain their voices. The club houses are still there, but the joogos (bocce courts) and passion have faded away with the previous generations of miners.

There were, also, baseball practices on the huge lawn of the Comerford Drive-in Theater across the highway from our home, where Dad seemed to enjoy hitting fly balls to me. Uncle Army (Armando) sometimes participated in the hitting too. There were also countless hunting trips with Dad, Sam, and my uncles once I was old enough to have a hunting license. I don't think I ever slept in the evening before a hunting trip.

Early one Sunday, Dad took me on a fishing excursion to the very remote north end of the Big Dam. We turned off Suscon Road onto Chapel Road and traveled about three miles south on a very primitive dirt road to an uninhabited shack that Dad called "Pinchko's Cabin." We parked the pickup and walked a worn path for about one-half mile. When we reached the point where Mill Creek flows into the reservoir, Dad suddenly swung the Fox shotgun from his shoulder and blasted a large pickerel for the catch-of-the day. Dad was a determined hunter and not a patient fisherman, but what happened on the path before we reached the creek was more bizarre. It was only minutes before daybreak and a mist enveloped the surrounding thick forest. As usual, Dad was on the hunt and the air was so silent that even a leaf hitting the ground probably could be heard. As I walked six or seven feet behind him carrying my fishing pole and bucket, we suddenly heard a slow rhythmic thumping that grew louder and increased to a very rapid frequency as it died away three or four seconds later. Dad yanked the lethal Fox fishing rod off his shoulder and stared intently into the mist, but resumed walking a minute later. The bizarre part was that I knew the sudden thumping that we both heard was not in the dense woods, but instead emanated from within my own eardrums! I was quite certain of it, but too startled to mention such a strange and crazy experience to him. Thanks to the Internet, I learned recently that there is a physiologic explanation called "Objective Pulsatile Tinnitus," which I never again experienced. Perhaps the event was not so crazy, after all and may even explain my tendency to motion sickness on amusement rides when I was young.

One Monday morning following a trip to Yankee Stadium, Dad emerged from the mine as I was running the mechanical loader and casually said he had to go some place. The rain jacket draped over his arm seemed a little odd; but nothing appeared wrong. When the miners emerged at the end of the day, I learned "some place" was the hospital, and the rain jacket hid a fractured wrist from me. When I arrived home that evening, Dad said he knew he was placing his arm in a dangerous position between the moving scoop and the roof of the mine, but the lack of sleep after our long trip to Yankee Stadium hindered his better judgment.

At this time, Dad and Gino started a mine on the outskirts of the small mining settlement of New Boston, which is one mile north of Old Boston, two miles south of Dupont, and on the east side of State Highway 315 (Location I in figure 1). I helped Dad drill and blast the rock to develop the pit. Each of us operated a compressed air jackhammer to drill vertically down into rock that was about thirty feet thick over the coal. See the third figure in figure 9 for a jackhammer drill. I would love to brag that I manhandled the heavy jackhammer; but it weighed approximately ninety pounds and had to be lifted about six feet high to position it over the drill hole. Dad would leave his jackhammer, start each drill hole for me, turn the jackhammer over to me to operate, and then return to his own jackhammer. One day, he positioned me far from the drill holes and detonated the thirty or forty dynamite-filled drill holes with a blasting plunger, while crouching under a truck-mounted air compressor. A rock about the size of a soft ball bounced under the truck and struck him just above the knee. Fortunately, the injury was not serious, but he limped for several days on a severely swollen leg.

The vein in New Boston was about 4-1/2 feet thick and the mine sloped down to the west under Highway 315. Dad pushed as hard as ever. He could often hear the distant rumbling of the steam shovel from inside the mine, and as soon as he heard it die away, he knew I was through pitching boney off the truck and sounded the bell in the shanty to signal me to start the loader. A few seconds later as Uncle Elmo pulled away and I scurried up the side of the pit to the shanty, he would ring the bell again. Although he was quite stern, Dad never once raised a hand to me and hardly ever had to yell. As soon as I heard his message, I moved. He would often say, "Run, don't walk!" Forty years later, Aunt Dorthea said she could still picture me, "Running to Dad's direction," one day when she saw us working around our home, but just think about it: isn't that the way *anyone* would respond to Superman?

I had become quite proficient in the operation of the mechanical loader and Dad also began to give me opportunities to operate the Caterpillar bulldozer, which was similar to the one shown in figure 10. One day, he instructed me to drive it about two miles up a dirt road from Yatesville (center of figure 1) , across Highway 315, and an additional one-half mile to the mine in New Boston. Running the big dozer down the dirt road was exhilarating, especially after I threw it into third gear. I always enjoyed running heavy equipment and once even volunteered to load an impatient driver's coal truck with the steamshovel, when Uncle Elmo had not yet returned from his haul. I had never operated a steamshovel before and can still see the look of regret on the driver's face as I banged the side of his truck box with the bucket.

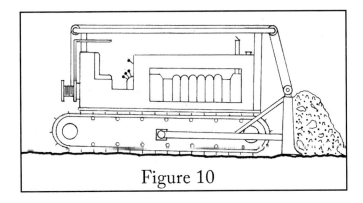

Figure 10

On the day I drove the dozer to New Boston, Dad was waiting for me when I arrived on the west side of Highway 315. He stopped the traffic and placed wood planks on the pavement so the dozer's steel cats would not damage it and continued on to other business after I crossed the highway. As I was going down a dirt road in New Boston, I was nervous because the blade on the front of the dozer barely fit between the wire fences that lined the yards of homes on each side. As the dozer crawled near one of the homes, an elderly woman followed alongside, waving her arms frantically and crying at the same time. I learned later that her husband was extremely ill in bed, upset by the roar of the ground-shaking dozer, and he died days or weeks later. In recent years, the homes have been replaced by a large warehouse complex and the little settlement of New Boston no longer exists.

Now that I was a little older, my fear of bears and snakes around the shanty was replaced by a slight touch of boredom. On one occasion, I stepped onto the top of the loader, gripped the rafters of the shanty, and attempted to operate the two levers of the loader with my feet. I am most certain Dad was not at the mine that day, and thankfully, no miners ever spotted me. I discontinued that dangerous practice within a few days. I also got into a little trouble when I decided to drive Dad's pickup back and forth on the dirt road leading to the mine, while he and the other miners were underground. As we drove home that day, I slumped in my seat and out of the corner of my eye, froze as I watched his puzzled expression gradually turn to anger as it slowly dawned on him that the imprint of fresh truck treads running up and down the steep side slopes of the dirt road were from his own pickup. It was the last time I drove his truck without his permission until I received my driver's license three years later.

One day, Dad said that the federal mine inspector would be paying us a visit that week and I should keep my eyes open for any unidentifiable cars coming up the dirt road. When I saw the vehicle, I was to sneak out the small hole through which the mechanical loader's cables passed through the front wall and sit some distance away from the shanty. Unfortunately, the inspector spotted me as he drove up the road. After he got out of his car, he said angrily, "I saw you sneaking out of the shanty! Get your father out of the mine!" When Dad came out, he sat quietly outside the mouth of the mine and the inspector proceeded to chew him out. He threatened Dad with severe penalties, and that was the end of my mining career, for about one or two weeks. The original notification by the inspector of his pending visit also alerted Dad to the hasty need for more mine props. Undoubtedly, state and federal mine inspection protocol during that period could have been improved.

At the New Boston mine, I witnessed another sight I will never forget. I followed Gino down to the mine entrance, but I myself had no need or intention to enter. As I sat on the ground near the entrance, Gino looked at the roof just before crawling into the mine and said, "Wait, kid! Back up! We're going to have a little excitement!" I glanced up at the roof and I could see the rock checker boarding. In the short period of two or three seconds, I watched the cracks in the roof proliferate rapidly until about three or four tons of rock suddenly crashed to the floor of the mine, just a few feet in front of us. Gino climbed over the rock pile laughing and, as he descended the slope, was singing improvised lyrics about his worthless life, comparing its meager value to a plugged nickel. I often heard miners talk about the importance of keeping an eye on the roof as they traveled underground, and the practice paid off big time for Gino that day.

As much as I admired them, miners occasionally made me the target of their jokes. Gino once laughingly asked me, in very explicit (and unprintable) terms that I had never heard before, about the extent of my sexual experience with women. At age thirteen, I only knew that women existed and they were suspiciously different. His exact words, as I (much) later learned, were quite raunchy and inappropriate, even in *Anthracite Grade*

School. When I went home that evening, I quoted Gino and asked Mother what this meant. She became very upset and strongly admonished that I should never use those words again. The next day, Gino said Dad had thoroughly chewed him out, and Gino shook his head in total amazement at my lack of awareness in this subject.

About the same time, I again found myself in a similar position of embarrassment. One day, the mechanical loader was silent because Dad and two other miners were setting props and attending to other dead work. Since they were only about 100 feet inside, I went down and sat near the mine entrance to pass time listening to the conversations. One miner was bragging about a recent conquest in bed with some woman. I sat there and listened intently (without understanding any of it) as he shared all of the most intimate details with Dad and another miner. At that instant, Dad suddenly suspected there might be an unexpected listener, hushed the miner, and subtly called out my name. After I responded hesitantly, the mine suddenly fell silent, except for the clanking of the shovels and saws. On another day, Dad and Sam were talking about hunting dogs and I inquired about how it was possible to distinguish between a male and female dog. Both laughed and Sam exclaimed, "You pick it up by the tail and smell it!" When they were through laughing, Sam said, "Someday, I'm going to tell you a little secret about life that's going to leave you with your mouth wide open and in shock!" To say that I was naïve on this particular subject for a thirteen-year-old would be a gross understatement. Using a slang sometimes heard from my Italian ancestors to describe a grossly unaware person, I was probably a gnocco (Nee–oo'- co), that is, a potato dumpling.

CHAPTER IX

EXETER (1955)

The location of this mine was near the base of the mountain on the west side of the Wyoming Valley and about 1/4 mile southwest of the Fox Hill Country Club and Golf Course in West Pittston (it was at location A in figure 1). Here, Dad mined the thickest, most beautiful vein of coal I had ever seen. It was extremely hard anthracite, and when two chunks bumped, it made a sound very similar to the sound that two glass bottles make when bumped together lightly, hence, the anthracite nickname, "Bottle Coal." Unfortunately, there was a major drawback with this bonanza that was not apparent when Dad first placed his dragline on the existing farmland and began digging down to the vein, i.e., *water*. The location was on the east side of Slocum Avenue in a low-lying area, and runoff from surrounding hills during rainstorms found its way to this location. With the dragline, he excavated a pit about 150 feet square and 50 feet deep into the clay, which was above the 10 or 15 feet of bedrock that covered the vein. Then, heavy rains saturated the Wyoming Valley. The farm soil was loose and a sub-surface stream began filling the pit with water. Dad traced the course of the hidden stream to a point about 200 feet away where the water was passing below the surface, through a shallow layer of loose mine rock left by a colliery that once operated nearby. With the dragline, he dug a trench in the mine rock about 10 feet wide by 8 feet deep and 50 feet long to expose the subsurface stream. See figure 11 for a dragline similar to Dad's. As he dug the trench, Dad dumped the rock as far as the dragline could reach; however, he directed me to push it even further away with the caterpillar dozer. At one point, I turned the caterpillar sideways on a steep side slope where the dozer felt ready to topple on its side if I moved another foot forward or back. Dad was annoyed and yelled, "What the hell are you doing? Are you trying to tip it over?" He straightened the machine out and I learned another valuable lesson in Anthracite Grade School.

At the bottom of the trench, the stream was exposed and flowing on firm clay. Dad cast farm soil in the trench in thin, even layers, leveling and compacting each layer in succession with the caterpillar to build a clay cut-off wall to stop the flow of the water. To this day, I marvel at Dad's intelligence and energy in developing makeshift solutions, which trained engineers take years to learn. The resulting clay barrier was impervious to the stream, and flow into the mine pit 200 feet away ceased, but the pit was now 3/4 filled with water. The average guy likely would have rented a large pump for several days to remove the water from the pit, but Dad wasn't the average guy.

The next day, after cutting off the flow of water to the pit, Dad borrowed an unusual hand auger from someone. I had never seen one like it before, and it resembled a carpenter's brace and bit used to bore a hole into wood.

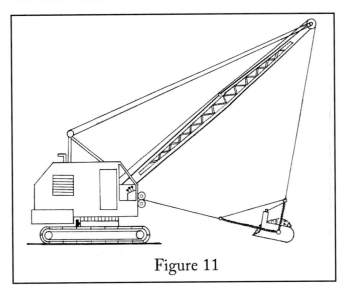

Figure 11

See the first drill in figure 9 for such a hand auger. However, this particular one had a very large crank, which two miners standing face-to-face could push and pull to advance the auger ten or twelve feet horizontally into the vein of coal. No doubt, it was the tool used by miners before electric drills were invented, and Dad did not yet have electric power at this site. Dad and I entered an old abandoned mine in a wooded area about 800 feet northeast of the pit and 500 feet south of the

present-day Fox Hill Country Club (the mine entrance
was at location B and Fox Hill is at C in Figure I). It
certainly was the nearest Dad ever got to a golf course
or country club. I did not have a helmet or headlamp,
and I followed him to a point he estimated was below
or very near the water-filled pit. We faced each other so
that my right hand was on one crank handle near his
left hand and my left hand was on the other handle to
his right. As we cranked, the auger advanced laterally
and upward to my right and it took, perhaps, one or two
hours to drill three holes. The vein was six feet thick,
but standing on loose coal or rock, my head rubbed
the sandstone roof. Water was dripping from the
roof and my red hunting cap was covered with muck,
which miners often referred to as "soapstone." Dad was
perturbed that I was ruining a perfectly good hunting
cap, but realized it was unavoidable. He packed the
drill holes with extra high explosive dynamite, which
he referred to as "gelatin," and ran a wire from the
exploder caps out toward the mine entrance. The wire
fell 100 to 150 feet short of the entrance, so Dad led
me outside before returning back inside to the end of
the wire to detonate the drill holes with a twist battery.

When we checked the pit, it was obvious the
explosion failed to burst through the sandstone roof. The
next day, however, after all the gases from the explosion
cleared, Dad returned back into the abandoned mine
to where we had drilled and filled the blasted cavity
near the mine roof with more gelatin. The resulting
explosion burst through the floor of the pit and drained
the water into the abandoned mine. The next step was

even more difficult than the previous one, for the clay mud now had to be removed from the pit. When such excavation occurs underground, miners refer to it as mucking. In the process of excavating the muck with the dragline, the bucket, which was capable of lifting five or six tons, sunk deeply into the mud and became stuck. The dragline did not have enough weight or power to free the bucket. Again, the average guy would likely rent a mobile crane service to free the bucket, but that wasn't Dad's way.

Instead, Dad turned the front of the crawler tracks so they were pointing toward the pit and so that the machine's heavy counterweight was at the back end of the crawler treads, which can be seen in figure 11. He then tensioned and locked the vertical hoisting cable so that the vertical resistance of the mired bucket lifted and held the back end of the dragline's crawler treads about three or four feet off the ground, and the front end of the treads pivoted into the ground near the pit. By this process, the weight of the tipped dragline was applying constant lift to the bucket through the vertical hoist cable, while Dad also applied the horizontal drag cable in an attempt to both lift and pull the bucket out of the mud. When he tried to pull the bucket forward, however, it would only advance a few inches, the front end of the crawler treads slid closer to the edge of the pit, and the back end of the crawler treads gradually settled to the ground. Then Dad would apply vertical lift to the bucket to again lift the rear end of both crawler treads off the ground before pulling the drag cable forward in another attempt to free the bucket. Dad repeated the same dangerous technique several times, and the front edge of the crawler treads slid closer to the edge of the pit each time. Instead of sitting in the operator's seat as he fought with the controls, he stood erect, prepared to jump if the machine suddenly slid or toppled into the pit. To add to my fear, the slanted dragline's cab door kept rolling forward and clanging shut so that he had to reopen it each time to keep his jump route clear.

Now, in the years I worked with Dad, I never once heard him utter a single curse word, that is, in English. When a machine did not do what he wanted, however, the Italian threats to the demons inside the machine flowed like the Susquehanna River. His favorites were something about "San Triste Mei' Troyya!" the "Putanna de la Troyya!" or similar "Pocca Putannas!." It sounded like a beautiful operatic aria, and as he knew, I did not understand the words at all; however, I was well aware that it was no "Pagliacci." As he battled with the dragline's controls, alternatively glaring at the bucket and the sky, the flow of perverse lyrics was nonstop, and I froze in anticipation of disaster. The sun was directly above the machine and I most certainly had a dazed, mouth open expression, as I squinted into the bright sunlight toward the steeply tipped dragline pivoted at the edge of the pit. Dad interrupted his barrage of putannas briefly to turn to me in the midst of his battle and yelled, "What the hell are you laughing at?" Rest assured, I hardly found this scene the least bit humorous, but after a long monumental battle that, to me, made Iwo Jima look like a Boy Scout troop picnic, the bucket finally broke free. Once the coal was loaded, a certain amount of mud content was inevitable, and the weighmaster's dockage was nearly as brutal as Dad's attack on the demons in the dragline.

Draglines struck me as being nearly as dangerous as underground mines. Once when Dad was walking the huge machine up a steep hill, he would swing the bucket ahead up the hill and dig it into the ground so the heavy dragline could pull itself up the incline with the drag cable. Once the machine crawled up the hill to the bucket and Dad continued to hold the dragline in that position, the crawler tracks needed to be locked so that the dragline would not shoot back down the hill when he again lifted the bucket. Once the tracks were locked, he could lift the three cubic yard bucket, again embed it further up the hill, and continue the climb after the tracks were again unlocked. Two levers that looked like sledgehammers were located between the crawler treads under the counterweight at the rear of the dragline. (See figure 11.) The most daunting task of my mining career was to crawl under the counterweight and roaring engine of the slanted dragline to adjust these hammer locks up and down each time Dad stopped and restarted up the hill. In another scenario, at the New Boston mine pit on the east side of Highway 315, the tall boom of the dragline swung back and forth immediately under a high voltage transmission line that still crosses 315 near there today. In order to escape the freezing temperatures one winter day, I huddled inside the cab next to the warm engine, as Dad dug the pit and swung the boom back and forth under the power line with a few feet to spare.

Additionally, I often wondered how Dad knew the steep side-slopes were strong enough to support the 96-ton weight of the machine just a few feet from the edge of the pit. After all, Dad was super-intelligent, but not a geotechnical engineer.

Dad and Gino experienced two dragline accidents during the 1950s. On the mountainside west of Old Forge, a brand-new dragline ran out of control down a hillside, toppled, and the operator from Old Forge had a serious back injury. At a colliery west of Keystone, the operator from Keystone toppled a dragline into a deep ravine, but escaped uninjured. Mining equipment of that era tended to be unsafe compared to the newer technology available today. One can go online and view numerous photos of toppled, crumpled draglines at mine pits.

For three or four months at the Exeter mine, bottle coal production with the mechanical loader in the six-foot high vein was outstanding. The miners were now robbing pillars, which was very productive because the pulley jack and tail rope cable could be easily positioned behind the blasted pillars. It was also very dangerous because the roof of the mine usually squeezed downward gradually as supporting pillars were robbed or reduced in size. A retired miner once proudly boasted how he saved time and money as loose coal spalled off the face of squeezing pillars, thereby eliminating the need to drill and blast the coal. At first, I thought his story was more boast than fact because I had never heard of this very dangerous mining technique. Then I recalled a scene in "The Molly Maguires" when a miner collected his pay at the end of a work week. The paymaster summarized the tons of coal the miner had loaded, calculated gross pay based on that weight, and then subtracted the cost of household and mining supplies purchased by the miner at the company store. The meager net pay may have been the incentive miners in an earlier era had for working in a squeezing mine with spalling coal pillars, to reduce the time and cost of drilling, i.e., so called dead work for which they were not paid.

As work progressed at the Exeter mine, Hurricane Diane hit the Wyoming Valley, and the farmer near the mine called Dad that evening to say a stream of water was running into the mine entrance. Around midnight, Dad, Uncle Elmo, and I went to the mine with Uncle Elmo's truck and began dragging the mechanical loader, steam shovel, and other equipment up the steep road out of the pit, as the hurricane raged and water streamed into the mine from one corner of the pit. After pulling the equipment up the steep road out of the pit, the three of us rode the truck to Moosic to view other damage along the Lackawanna River. The next day after the storm, the pit appeared dry, but the Exeter mine was almost totally plugged with clay, sand, and silt, and had to be abandoned. Dad had been noticeably subdued when we toured storm damage along the Lackawanna River in the previous evening; but he never seemed deterred or discouraged when such setbacks occurred at his mines. When he drilled and loaded solid rock for weeks in the gangway at the Yatesville mine (figure 1) without finding the main vein is another example of such a setback. The major accidents to the draglines in Keystone and Old Forge are also examples of setbacks where a barrage of angry putanna arias was certain, but not despair. I did see occasional tears from Dad, but they were all from uncontrollable laughter, not despair.

Many years later, during one of the countless stories we exchanged about the mines, my father-in-law recalled working underground in the general area of the Exeter mine, and water draining off the mountain on the west side of the valley was a major problem at his mine also. This is one example of the mundane topics ex-miners like to rehash. In recent years, the farmland around the former Exeter Mine has been developed into residential housing, and as could be predicted, the partially uncovered mine pit has been integrated into the development's storm water collection system.

CHAPTER X

YATESVILLE (1956-57)

I was proud of my role in helping Dad start the mine in Yatesville. (See location G in figure 1 for this location.) He took me along one evening when he visited the man who owned the leased rights to the coal to obtain approval to start the mine. Mike, who lived in Yatesville, was very ill in bed with black lung disease. He could hardly speak, but before we left, he talked about his passion for accordion music and asked me to learn to play an old John Phillip Sousa march that he himself used to play called "Under the Double Eagle." About one week later, we returned with my accordion and I played the march five or six times, and lying in bed with a huge grin, his eyes swelled with tears. Within days, Dad started the new mine, but Mike requested that Dad install a mine hoist, tipple, and gangway. After revealing the vein with the bulldozer on the side of a hill, Dad and another miner, Bruno, began blasting the rock and coal, and hoisting it to the tipple. Following standard procedure, a cut of coal was removed from the top half of the tunnel, and then rock was cut from the bottom half. At a large colliery, rock was usually dumped separately into a truck on a sidetrack near the tipple by a piece of equipment oddly nicknamed a Mary Ann. At Dad's tipple, Uncle Elmo hauled coal and rock separately as each was cut sequentially. The coal was poor quality and was temporarily stockpiled until it could be mixed with the good coal when the main vein was reached. Although the vein was only about three feet thick and extremely soft, Dad assumed it was the outcrop and guessed that extending the gangway would soon lead to the main vein and high quality anthracite. He and Bruno struggled in the tunnel for several weeks and probably looked with envy at a coal tipple and mine operated by Mike's son 800 feet away, down in the flat valley where the vein was high and easily reached. Mike had given Dad a much more difficult mining lease, but under these circumstances, nepotism was certainly understandable.

For a few days, I worked in the gangway with Dad and Bruno as a car topper. As they shoveled the blasted rock into the mine car, I would also toss in small slabs. As the loaded rock reached the top of the car, I would ring the four edges of the mine car with rock slabs to build a sort of retaining wall. I built the walls as rapidly as they shoveled and recall Dad and Bruno smiling at each other without saying a word because with the aid of my rock walls, the topping was climbing substantially above the mine car's sideboards. Years later, my father-in-law told me about a hardworking car topper who built up the sides so quickly, the exhausted miners threw their shovels at the topper and yelled, "The car is full!" In earlier years, miners were paid for each car loaded and overly exuberant car toppers were not appreciated. At Dad's mines, men were usually paid the same daily rate regardless of quantity mined.

Unfortunately, the gangway in the Yatesville Mine had progressed to a length of around 100 feet, but the grade and thickness of the coal were not improving, because we had not found the true outcrop. One day while searching the surrounding woods, Dad found the real outcrop about 500 feet from the mouth of the tunnel. I could have kicked myself because I, too, had seen this outcrop when tramping around the woods in prior days, but neglected to bring it to Dad's attention. It was probably my greatest personal disappointment of all my mining experiences. Dad abandoned the gangway, but about fifty years later, I revisited this site. The tunnel was overgrown with trees and bushes and the deteriorated mine car was nearby, still serving as my personal sentimental anthracite museum.

After abandoning the tunnel, Dad began to widen the newly found outcrop with the caterpillar and excavate the storage pit for the steam shovel. On occasion, Dad left the mine to tend to his other enterprises and directed me to operate the dozer in his absence. I was probably only five or six years old when I first operated a bulldozer, that is, for three or four minutes while sitting on Dad's lap. As mentioned earlier, I enjoyed any opportunity to run the machine. I think he was pleased with my proficiency with the machine that day in 1957 and told me so when he saw the volume of rock I had moved. Once the pit was dug, steam shovel and mechanical loader installed, the miners went to work and I continued my usual responsibilities for running the loader and removing boney from Uncle Elmo's truck. By this time, he and Dad had traded the old green Brockway for a 1954 F-900 Z-license Ford with the same eleven- or twelve-ton capacity. The Ford was much lighter, however, so that my uncle no longer had to fear the state police mobile truck scales and the jail in Dupont. Uncle Elmo's deteriorated dump truck, now sixty years old, rests in a wooded gulley in another personal anthracite museum on the south side of a two-lane paved road in Laflin.

Dad and Gino were now broadening their operations. They were operating dogholes in Irish Hill, New Boston, and Yatesville. They also opened a coal reclamation process whereby small-sized anthracite previously wasted near breakers became as valuable, or more so, than mined coal. With the advent of new household stoker furnaces around 1950, small anthracite grades called rice and buckwheat were now in demand. This coal was on the surface, easy to access and load using a piece of equipment miners called a grizzly, and only had to be screened one final time and washed at the breaker. It could be found on the surface at the site of abandoned breakers, old railroad beds, and landfills. Decades earlier, it had also been flushed thru boreholes back into abandoned veins, where miners now returned to mine it a second time. Dad also collected rent from the restaurant and home above it and had built Mother's dream home on a hill behind the restaurant. The home and restaurant were on the east side of State Route 315, one mile south of Dupont (location J in figure I). The state eventually purchased these properties in 1962, before building Interstate 81 with an access ramp that intersected Highway 315 at this location.

Despite his growing success, Dad was still driven to take advantage of any small financial opportunity that presented itself. One day, a pile of old abandoned cast-iron parts and fittings lay strewn along a dismantled railroad track. After loading the pickup, we hauled the scrap metal to a local recycling shop where Dad probably received twenty or thirty dollars. A few days later, I also helped Dad load and recycle the steel fishplates that were about one foot square, one inch thick, and used to anchor a steel railroad track to the wood cross-ties with thick steel spikes. This was the same rail track behind his Old Boston homestead where twenty-five to thirty-five years earlier, Nonna would lead her children to throw and gather chunks of anthracite off the tops of large slow-moving coal cars. This type of coal boot-legging was quite common during the Great Depression and can still be seen in historical documentaries about the Wyoming Valley where mothers and children are filmed running away from a slow moving train and the incriminating eye of the camera. In Irish Hill, the water company had abandoned a buried twelve- or sixteen-inch diameter cast iron pipe. In quick succession starting at one exposed end, Dad used a heavy jack to lift each pipe section up out of the ground and then shattered each pipe section with a sledgehammer. I helped load the pieces in the pickup and we hauled them to the recycling yard.

Years later, it occurred to me that the cast iron and fishplates may or may not have been truly abandoned. In the worst case, I reasoned that like Nonna's boot-legging, our recycling may have been fair retribution to the railroad industry that blatantly exploited immigrant miners fifty years earlier during the Anthracite Revolution. The bottom line is that recycling ventures like these were a holdover from Dad's difficult childhood and the deprivation of the Great Depression twenty-five years earlier. Certainly, Dad was not cold and hungry at this point, nor did he any longer need to hand-carry water out of the mine with two buckets, but the effects of those difficult years were embedded in him for his entire life.

Quite often, Dad would use the money from recycled metals to throw an unscheduled picnic for the miners. On more than one occasion, the grimy group would emerge from the mine, sprawl on the ground, and enjoy a feast of homemade red wine, bread, provolone, prosciutto, porquetta, or loansa, with hot green and red cherry peppers. During one such feast and as the wine flowed, the group of four or five exhausted miners sat on the side of a railroad track near the mine in Yatesville and playfully argued whether the track was straight or crooked.

Camaraderie among the miners was unique. They partied, cried, and joked together. When it came to jokes, Dad often pushed everyone's limit of endurance.

On one occasion, he removed a dead dog from the highway in front of the restaurant, took it to the mine, and placed it under the hood of one miner's car. When the miner returned to work on Monday morning, he complained to another unsuspecting miner that he had taken his family to Rocky Glen Amusement Park on Sunday and could not find the source of the foul odor. The other miner helpfully inquired if he had checked under the hood. At that point, I thought it best to turn and walk toward the shanty and could not hear what was transpiring because their voices behind me were drowned out by a nearby air compressor. Approaching the shanty, I looked back at the miners to see that the car hood was wide open, they were standing about twenty-five feet away from it and waving their arms as they argued. Around the same time, Dad bet another miner ten dollars that he could strike the headlight of the miner's old pickup with a rock from a distance of about thirty feet, and the miner accepted the bet. Dad underhanded a round rock, palm down like a bocce ball with which he was highly skilled, and shattered the headlight. When my sister was in the tenth grade, a classmate came courting and Dad pretended to turn him away sternly at the front door while wielding the double barrel.

Invariably, everyone would break out in laughter after the prank, but Dad much more so than the victim. Once, while he was loading a truck with the dragline, he hoisted a bucket of coal to the top of the truck and asked the driver to climb into the bucket to toss out a large slab of rock. While the trucker was inside the bucket, Dad lifted and held it about four feet above the truck. Dad looked down at me from his seat in the dragline as tears of laughter rolled down his cheeks and as the driver clutched the sides of the bucket in terror.

Through the years, I had heard of similar questionable pranks pulled long ago by his father and believe Dad inherited the gene from Nonno and continued to cultivate it. Apparently, Nonno's pranks were even more questionable than Dad's. Based on innuendo, Nonno's daughters, who refused to cry at his funeral in 1941, were some of his favorite targets. Recently, I have concluded that Nonno's pranks, while both extreme and humorously intended, were rooted in the same stern demeanor that was so critical to his survival underground and necessary to his family's evolution during a very difficult economic period. Perhaps it's just a guy thing, but it's my explanation and I am sticking with it.

They say, "Apples don't fall far from the tree," as if I should have been so lucky, but now that I think of it, I too pursued the prank gene and may have even surpassed Dad and Nonno on two occasions. When I was a senior in high school, my little sister and I were home alone late one evening when she bolted out of her dark bedroom, ran into the TV room where I was sitting, and cried, "Something is tapping on my window!" I replied, "Don't cry. It's just Nunzio." Nunzio was my good friend in high school. In the dark bedroom, I cranked the window open, poked the 12-gage double barrel into the darkness, blasted two shots, and then in mock anger yelled, "Who's out there?" Nunzio later reported the gun barrel was only a short distance above his head, and in the darkness, the flame out of the end of the barrel was two feet long. Following another evening of fun and frolic in the twelfth grade, I apologetically announced to classmates Nunzio and Tom that I would not stop in front of their houses in Inkerman (bottom left corner of fig. 1), but they would need to hastily disembark my 1952 Plymouth as it coasted along in second gear. The sight of Nunzio desperately avoiding trees opposite his house, as he dashed through the woods to catch up to his momentum, is forever etched in my memory. Obviously, these pranks were far too dangerous, and I am happy to report that my pranks in recent years have reached a much higher level of maturity. More importantly, Nunzio and Tom are still good friends, and because of my thoughtful coaching, both became more athletic and Nunzio learned how to use doorbells.

Tossing theirs caps in the air and shooting at them with their rifles, wrestling, and other playful games were also common among the miners. They called one unusual game "chiqueta." Each miner would take a bocce ball and throw it underhanded as far as they could along Old Boston Road, which forms a horseshoe about one mile in total length, to see whose toss would roll furthest. The road was not paved as it is now, but probably held the national record at that time for number of potholes per mile of road. The game would proceed from one end of the settlement to the other and returned to the Old Boston Club House near the south end of the horseshoe. The miner with the fewest winning throws when they returned to the clubhouse had to buy the beer.

CHAPTER XI

TRUCKS, DOZERS, AND A TREACHEROUS MINE (1958)

I continued to operate the mechanical loader and pitch boney off the haul trucks at the various dogholes during the summer, school vacations, and on weekends. At Irish Hill, I helped Dad build an elevated wood ramp from the entrance of the mine up to a point where the truck could be loaded directly by the mechanical loader so that a steam shovel was not necessary. Dad's creativity in solving mining problems was remarkable. There was not any deliberation, planning, sketching, or carpenter's assistance. He built tunnels, tipples, ramps, shanties as if naturally driven. Bruno was the foreman for the new Irish Hill mine, and Dad paid him for each truckload of loaded coal. He was a lifelong friend, and I even named my hunting dog Bruno instead of Nunzio, but friendship aside, Bruno became annoyed with me whenever I overloaded the truck. Nevertheless, I knew how my bread was buttered and routinely heaped the coal truck with the mechanical loader. Since the coal there was a lower quality, it was trucked approximately two to three miles to the west and mixed with the high quality coal at the New Boston mine. After mixing, it would benefit from the higher price received for the New Boston coal. The haul was over a treacherous pioneer road at about five or ten miles per hour, curving around and over hills and adjacent to abandoned deep strip mines.

After I loaded (heaped) the final truckload one day with the mechanical loader, I was anxious to get behind the wheel of the Ford F-900 dump truck, and I persuaded Bruno to let me haul the load to New Boston. Very reluctantly but probably anxious to go home, Bruno relented. Approximately one-half way down the pioneer road, I encountered a drainage swale in the road, which I knew would tip the top-heavy truck precariously, no matter how slowly I negotiated it. At the last minute, I elected to steer down a parallel, but unused trail that was flat, but muddy. The truck bogged down, was axle deep in the mud, and wheels spun without moving forward. This would certainly have been an appropriate time for some putanna arias, but fortunately, I never picked up on that part of Dad's training. A cell phone also would have been helpful, but they didn't exist at that time and I still do not have one! I kneeled down in the mud and began scooping it away from the tires and axle with my arms. After about sixty minutes of crawling in and clearing the muck, I saw Dad speeding and bouncing up the trail in his brand-new black 1958 Lincoln. He had showered, dressed, and apparently was headed for the Old Boston Clubhouse before he called Bruno to find out why I had not yet returned home. From a distance beyond the quagmire, he sounded more upset than relieved, but from the way he sped up the pioneer trail with the Lincoln, I suspect the opposite was true. He yelled that he was going for the bulldozer and slowly drove away. I continued to pull the mud from around the tires and axle with my arms and drove the truck out of the marsh just as Bruno arrived. Neither Dad nor Bruno ever said anything more about the event, but personally, I thought I demonstrated some pretty good mucking and trucking skills.

On another day, Bruno had driven Dad's pickup to the mine in Irish Hill, and at the end of the work day, I again coaxed Bruno to let me drive it home. He reluctantly sat on the rider's side as I drove along the dirt road from Irish Hill and then down Suscon Road. A fresh snow had fallen and the paved road leading three miles west from Suscon to Dupont was icy. About 2-1/2 miles east of Dupont (figure I), the pavement descends a steep hill for about 1/4 of a mile. Near the bottom of the hill, two or three vehicles were stalled at the side of the road and drivers were standing near their vehicles. As we descended the hill, the pickup began sliding and gyrating from side to side. For some strange reason that I still do not fully understand, I laughed uncontrollably as the pickup slid faster and sideways between the stalled vehicles, barely clearing them on either side. Bruno swore later that one of the stranded drivers peed his pants as we skidded past. It was one of those occasions when I like to think that my trucking skills bailed me out again, but Bruno did not agree. Nevertheless, Dad may have been impressed by my driving skills or my enthusiasm to drive coal trucks, and one day shortly after receiving my driver's license, allowed me to haul coal from the mine in Yatesville to the #9 Breaker in Hughestown (figure I). I made seven trips that day with a Ford F-900 dump truck and blasted the air horn each time I passed Uncle Elmo going in the opposite direction.

The mine in Yatesville (location G in figure 1) was positioned between two railroad tracks that crossed to form an "X." The coal outside the "X" had been strip-mined years earlier by another company; but not near or under the "X" because of the interference of the two railroads. The new mine tunnel sloped steeply from the outcrop down the hillside to the railroad and then turned left to parallel under the railroad at the base of the hill. The layout had great advantages and disadvantages. The advantage was that as the main tunnel was advanced along the base of the hill, side chambers were blasted back up the hill, and each cut of coal naturally slid down into the tunnel. Sheet metal was anchored between the props so that almost the entire cut of coal slid to where the loader could easily scoop it out to the pit. The disadvantage, as the miners reported, was that the mine rumbled and shook each time a train passed overhead, threatening a roof collapse. The vein was 4 to 4-1/2 feet high and the hard coal sold at the breaker for about $6.50 per ton. As I can recall, prepared anthracite sold to homeowners at around $20 per ton. Despite the difficult conditions, Dad decided to open another mine about 500 feet away, very near the intersection of the two railroad tracks, one of which has since been dismantled. After starting the excavation, Dad directed me to continue removing the rock with the caterpillar each afternoon at the new site, while he and the other miners drilled the next cut of coal and set props in the existing mine. When he emerged from the mine at the end of each day, I recall how pleased he was with the progress I was making with the caterpillar.

The new mine tunnel was slanted from right to left, and after progressing forty or fifty feet horizontally, began also sloping steeply downward. The treachery of these conditions are truly impossible to diagram, but see figure 12 for an innocuous view. Miners traveled through the mine by sliding from prop to prop. Although it was easier to walk along the bottom of the side-slope at the vein sidewall, or rib as miners called it, that was the more dangerous unpropped zone and travel path for the scoop. About seventy-five feet from the entrance, the vein's floor and roof came together and the vein terminated at what miners call a roll. Dad and Gino instinctively knew the vein must resume nearby because they could see where the vein had been strip-mined years earlier beyond the railroad track. They continued drilling and blasting through the rock for a few days and finally found the vein again. Now, however, the vein and tunnel continued to slope downward, but twisted from left to right. To make matters worse, air in the mine was bad until side chambers could be mined back up the sideslope to the outcrop and ventilate to the outside air. A safety lamp hung from a prop and a small flame flickered inside the glass enclosure to tell the miners that there was still enough oxygen near the face of the mine. If the flame was no longer visible, it was the signal to evacuate quickly because carbon dioxide was filling the chamber. The miners referred to this condition as "black damp," which, through the years, asphyxiated countless anthracite miners.

In the midst of their peril, miners seldom lost their sense of humor. On one occasion, the quality of the air in the mine, though adequate to keep the tiny flame in the safety lamp burning, was marginal and making it difficult to breathe. They instructed one young uneducated and inexperienced miner to grab a bunch of the small paper tamping bags, fill them with air at the entrance to the mine, and bring the air back to the face where the men were working. The miners laughed for days after the young man fell for the prank. They occasionally asked him to sing for them, which he did enthusiastically. "Cruising Down the River on a Sunday Afternoon" came out as, "Tuusing Down the River...." in a nonmusical monotone, and the humor helped the men endure the difficult working conditions.

At the end of one shift, however, Gino crawled out of the mine and standing, threw one glove ten feet into the air and then the other. When conditions in a mine were very tough, Gino would often say with pride, "I (physically) bulled through it." On this day, however, he continued to trudge in obvious frustration toward his pickup without saying a word. He did not want to make a living that way and for good reason. Even a minotaur would struggle in this doghole. To add to his dilemma, Gino's left hand was crippled since birth, and it prevented him from gripping a shovel and other tools properly and conveniently.

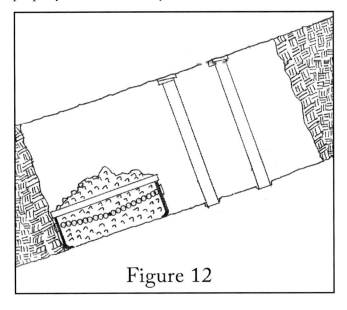

Figure 12

Twenty-five years later, however, he would own collieries, outdoor theaters, a hotel, and confide to me that his financial accounts were worth "thirteen big ones," as he put it. A "big one" was his slang for "one million dollars."

I can recall the strength and passion of the men who worked that mine, besides Dad and Gino. One can easily imagine that only the very strong ones stuck around. Ernie worked his own small dairy farm in Suscon (right side of figure 1) each evening after his shift at the mine. He was packed with muscle after a lifetime of hard labor. Dad said Ernie often snapped shovels after shoving them under and lifting large chunks of coal or rock. Even during normal conversation, his baritone voice resonated volume and power in an unusual way. Dad joked that when they were hunting and Ernie was booming his thundering yells through the woods to flush out deer, the deer were happy to be shot! When telling a story, Ernie would look close into my face and, with one eye closed like a pirate, emphasize his point by waving his right forefinger in my face and alternatively rapping his knuckles on my chest with the back of his same right hand. As if he had to impress me any further, he emerged from the mine one day and, in coal-crusted boots, clothes, helmet, and headlamp, did five push-ups at age forty-one or forty-two with one arm bent behind his back. When we visited him one evening while he was tending to his milk cows, he asked me to turn in the other direction so as to, in his words, "check something out" in the corner of the barn. Ernie then nailed the back of my neck with a powerful gush from one of the cow's utters. For days, no amount of scrubbing removed the raw milk's strange odor.

Bruno was another big strong miner from Keystone who liked to recount stories about his record of 9 and 1 as an amateur heavyweight boxer in the United States Navy. He would lift his head and pointing to his left nostril, display the bent septum received in his final bout. He worked very hard, and when he occasionally overslept, I would ride with Dad to Bruno's home in Keystone where Dad would knock on his door to wake him. Victor was another hardworking miner with brute strength and a great family man from Sebastapool, which is just south of Pittston. Our families occasionally enjoyed a cookout at Lake Wallenpaupak, or Nay Aug Park in Scranton, where Victor was usually the expert at roasting chickens on an open fire. Miners seemed to enjoy working with Dad and stuck with him for years. Some told me, however, they had never been pushed so hard. I am convinced they could tolerate it because although he pushed constantly, he did so respectfully and worked even harder alongside of them. He was also a great friend with a good sense of humor. Years later, I decided that his was the ideal style of leadership and people management. However, all of the miners were part of a special league, much like the "League of Miners" from Spoleto, of which I reported in chapter 2.

That summer, I had another memorable experience of a very different kind. I was practicing my accordion in the study room in the basement of our home, when the daughter of my parents' very close friends made a social visit. She came with her girl friend, and as I played a classic tune from the 1940s called "In The Mood," the two very attractive eighteen-year-olds, who had just graduated from Pittston High School, jitterbugged to the music. Suddenly, draglines, dozers, and big green Brockways lost their allure, and I realized, for the first time, pretty girls had a well-deserved place in this world. I hardly spoke to girls at school and recall going to only one high school dance. After the jitterbug, however, I began to view them in a different mood. As they say, "Better late than never!"

Nevertheless, her father frightened the heck out of me one evening when I overheard him tell my parents that during our upcoming vacation to Atlantic City, his daughter and I could go our own way at the shore while the two families vacationed. A day or two before the scheduled trip, I strongly insisted to my parents that I was not interested in Atlantic City and wanted to stay behind with Nonna where "I could make better use of my time." I probably spent my valuable time watching reruns of *Ramar of the Jungle* on TV or in some equally useless pastime. In retrospect, my meager social skills had probably caved in to my significant mining and trucking skills.

CHAPTER XII

GRADUATION (1959)

The year began to unfold with a series of sad events. The Susquehanna River broke into the Knox Mine (Location E in figure 1) just south of Pittston and twelve miners were forever entombed. I personally knew one of the deceased miners, a kind gentleman named Frank Burns, who occasionally inspected Dad's mine on behalf of the coal company that owned the leases to the coal. Dad's cousin, Joe Stella, survived and received an award for leading a group of trapped miners to an old abandoned air vent through which they vertically clawed their way to safety. Uncle Jim Musto escaped up one of the gangways just ahead of the rising water. It took more than one month for authorities to plug the gaping hole that was about thirty feet square in the river bottom, but by then, submerged veins from Scranton to Wilkes-Barre had to be abandoned because of the prohibitive cost of pumping the water. However, the entire event was overshadowed when our very good friend, Victor, was killed in a roof fall at Dad's mine in New Boston. Victor left behind a wonderful wife, son, and daughter.

Although I had been a successful student for three years at West Pittston High School, where my parents were paying my tuition so I could prepare for college, my grades suddenly deteriorated during the initial semester of my senior year. Inexplicably, school had become quite boring, and Dad was forced to transfer me to Jenkins Township High School (Location F in figure 1) to graduate. Near the same time, I told my parents that I did not want to go to college to be a doctor, but instead wanted to join the United States Marines. Looking back at all the disappointment I created, I am amazed that such a demanding father never punished me. I asked the marine recruiter to speak to Dad in an effort to obtain Dad's approval for me to enlist. The sergeant explained very diplomatically to Dad, "If he doesn't want to go to college now, he may feel differently after his four years of service. Besides, his test scores were very good and he qualifies for advanced technical training after boot camp." Dad relented and signed his approval.

My parents were terribly upset, but it was not long before Dad again displayed his unfaltering support, which in retrospect, I certainly had not earned. My new classmates soon learned of our cottage on the Lehigh River in Thornhurst and asked me to see if Dad would allow us to have a graduation party there. Mother was leery, but again Dad said, "They just want to have a little fun and some beer," and added emphatically, "But no girls!" The night of the party, one of the five or six girls there said, "Your dad just pulled up out front and wants to talk to you." Bruno was behind the wheel and Dad cranked the window down on the rider's side. Sternly, he said, "I thought I told you no girls!" I looked down at the ground without saying anything, and after a few uncomfortable seconds, Dad said, grinning, "Go get us 2 bottles of beer." In a few minutes more, he and Bruno drove off. I think he had concluded, accurately, "This is a good group of kids having clean fun," or perhaps he circled back later to double check. Years later, I vowed that I would be as supportive and lenient with my own teenagers as Dad and Mother were with me. My vow was tested subsequently when one son, Nick, returned to Arizona without my car after a trip to California where the car was impounded for illegal parking. Around the same time, my other son, Pete, sneaked off with my car and bumped our house when pulling back into our garage. When I purchased a beautiful red sports car for my daughter, Renee', when she turned seventeen, her only response was, "It has potential." In my opinion, I passed all the tests of my vow with flying colors and can report the three of them, today, would make any parent quite proud!

The photo on the next page with my hand on Dad's shoulder was taken at my going-away party in July of 1959, and the next day, my parents took me to the train station in Wilkes-Barre for the long trip to Marine Boot Camp at Parris Island, South Carolina. The recruiter

Louis Ronald Scatena

elected to publicize my enlistment, including a picture in the newspaper with Dad and I shaking hands before I boarded the train. In the photo, it appears obvious Dad is trying hard to smile.

During my second or third week of boot camp, Dad wrote a letter in which he told me about the latest events at home. His words were warm without a hint of emotional sentiment. Anthracite miners did not openly communicate emotion, at least not Dad. Besides, I was confident in our feelings toward each other, and spoken words were not necessary or mean anything more. At the end of his letter, he asked me if it was okay to invest the $3,500 that I had accumulated in our joint bankbook during the years he had paid me for my work at the mines and said he thought investing it in stock market blue chips might be a good idea. What I would pay today for a copy of that letter! It was the only time Dad had ever asked me for my permission to do anything. Perhaps in a state of shock, I wrote back with a touch of sarcasm that I regret to this day: "Yes, it's okay with me. Besides, I always regarded the money as more yours than mine." That certainly was a foolish statement on my part because there was absolutely no way Dad would take any of the money for his personal use. The stocks that he purchased under our joint names were the bluest of blue chips: American Telephone and Telegraph, Continental Can, and Keystone Custodian Stock Fund.

On September 9, 1959, I was in a prone position firing my M-1 rifle at targets on the rifle range, and I periodically glanced out of the corner of my eye toward my drill instructor approaching across a broad field. He was walking slowly with his head down. His demeanor was remarkably different from the animated, growling style I had witnessed over the prior six or seven weeks. He shuffled up and said, "Let's go. Your mother wants you home." Marine recruits do not ask questions, and without further explanation, the drill sergeant took me to the supply warehouse for a dress uniform and to the train depot in Yemesee. Although I had to make two or three train changes along the way, I never called home. Besides, I knew what had happened, but did not want to hear it. The next evening, as I got out of the taxi a few hundred feet from our house, two friends working at a nearby service station walked over to the taxi and said, "We're sorry. He was a great man," thereby confirming my worst fear. Our home was filled with family and friends, and since I had not eaten for some time, I rode with Uncle Nick to a curb-service diner on South Main Street, Pittston, where we ate sandwiches and cried together in his car.

Even with the benefit of hindsight, it is perplexing to see how Dad's plight, and that of more than 100,000 other anthracite miners, escaped them and their families before the inevitable occurred: explosions, dangerous equipment, roof collapses, black damp, black lung. Why be a miner, and why didn't we take more action to change their course? For these very unusual men, the answers may be embedded in chapters 2 and 3. Perhaps after 1940, the industry, more subtly, took advantage of ambitious young men the same way it lured immigrants forty to sixty years earlier. In addition to the tragic loss of Dad, Victor, and Frank Burns, I sadly witnessed two friends, Tucci and Nunzio's dad, desperately trying to breathe in the final throes of black lung disease. Although he died when I was only nine or ten, I still remember the large blue scar that Uncle Primo carried on the side of his forehead from a mine explosion.

The following is a list of the accidents, physical problems, and near misses that Dad endured from 1942 to 1959. The list is even more striking with the realization that these are only the incidents that I heard or witnessed. The complete list, if known, would likely be twice as long:

1942: A dump truck that he was driving at a mine on a steep hill in Mocanaqua lost its brakes and he jumped clear as it ran away.

1943: Received a broken leg in a mine accident and was on crutches for an extended period.

1948: Running a bulldozer on top of a hill behind Old Boston and jumped clear just before the dozer jumped out of gear and plunged into a deep strip mine.

1949: Accidentally swallowed fuel oil while siphoning from a fuel drum and became very ill.

1954: Fractured wrist between top of scoop and roof of mine when the scoop suddenly shifted.

1954: After pushing the plunger, a boulder blasted out of the strip mine, bounced under the truck that he assumed was shielding him, and struck his knee to cause severe swelling.

1954: Received bad burns on his hands after gripping power lines in the mine that supposedly had been turned off.

1955: Operated a dragline with the boom passing repeatedly under a high voltage power line. The boom of the dragline suddenly lurched and bumped the high voltage line, but he apparently was electrically grounded and unaffected by the large voltage that passed through him.

1955: Struggled to free a dragline from the mud and nearly tipped it into the stripping hole.

1957: Was prospecting for a coal mining opportunity in an abandoned mine in Old Forge. Encountered very bad air and barely made it back up the steep slope to fresh air.

1958: While running the bulldozer in a frigid blizzard, the steel cable that hoists the blade jammed in a pulley and he lost the tip of one finger when he suddenly freed the cable with his hands.

1958: Probably from excessive coal dust, had problem breathing freely, and a doctor had to chip away bone in a sinus or nostril passageway with a mallet and small medical chisel.

1959: Extensive shoulder pain and bursitis at age forty.

1959:   Killed in collapse of a mine roof in
        September in Yatesville.

EPILOGUE

My wife of fifty years, Frances, has been an outstanding partner and mother to our three children. Only in recent years has it dawned on me that her own family's direct connection to anthracite mining had been more than just a subtle attraction. One might conclude that my sense of values had been misplaced, but not if they fully understood my side of the connection. Whenever her parents would visit us in Arizona from their home in Exeter (upper left corner of figure 1), Pennsylvania, her Dad and I would remain at the kitchen table for hours and talk about the mines after she and her mother retired to the TV room. Pete's mine, the Diamond Colliery in West Scranton, employed more than 200 miners. He and I thoroughly enjoyed exchanging experiences and stories about anthracite mining in the Wyoming Valley. Big Pete had five for each of my own. Recently, I met another engineer who had a similar youthful experience in the mines of West Virginia. As he related his experience, his wife described the pride her husband demonstrated whenever he recounted such stories. Without similar experience and memories, it is most unlikely anyone can ever fully comprehend and appreciate the importance of that heritage to those affected.

It is likely that, if I had to spend my life as a miner, I would feel differently. As it turned out, the youthful experience of relatively short duration was just enough to incite fond memories. One of the drawbacks of dwelling on the past is that someone, as in my case, could become reluctant to experience some of the basic wonders of the modern world, e.g., ATMs, iPads, iPods, cell phones, etc., but as I humorously tell friends, "There's plenty of time to learn, if necessary." After all, I *did_*free an anthracite loaded dump truck buried in mud, without a call for help!

I graduated from engineering school in 1967, worked for an architectural and engineering firm in Scranton for eight years, and then for the large utility that provides water and power to Central Arizona. In 2003, I had an opportunity to retire from the utility with full benefits after twenty-eight years of service. Two weeks after retirement, I interviewed with a large engineering consulting firm in Phoenix. I explained to the committee of three interviewers that I had been out of engineering and in positions of management for the previous eighteen years, but would now like to continue my original career as a professional structural engineer. I assured them that despite lacking recent technical design experience, I could do the work to their satisfaction. As Uncle Ted and Dad had proposed to Barber Motors in Pittston in 1937, I proposed to my interviewers that I would be willing to work without pay for several weeks to demonstrate my aptitude and enthusiasm. In response, the lead interviewer said, "It's been my experience that when you pay nothing, you receive nothing in return. Therefore, we'll start you near the bottom of the pay grade for your position." He obviously was not aware of my extensive training in Anthracite Grade School. There was no way he would "receive nothing in return." After my achievements in engineering over the past eleven years, including several promotions and technical publications, he has a much better understanding. When asked if I plan to retire soon, I usually respond, "I'm just warming up! Besides, all the retired guys I know are dead!"

Before she passed away recently, Aunt Mary said, "Your dad taught you very well." Sometimes, I think he may have taught me too well, but I would not exchange the experience and memories of working at the mines with Dad for any treasure the world has to offer. Whenever I revisit the Wyoming Valley and see the huge wind turbines on the mountaintop slightly above and east of Irish Hill, I inevitably think of Dad and the other miners. Their images are as vivid as the turbines on the skyline, standing silent, tall, and strong.

GLOSSARY AND INDEX OF MINING TERMS

Black damp: Carbon dioxide in the form of a thin vapor that replaces oxygen in the mine chamber and asphyxiates the miner. (Page 110)

Bond (Strip-mine): A financial bond of several thousand dollars, which the mine operator legally posts in the name of the landowner. The bond is returned after the operator restores the surface of the ground to its original condition, at the end of mining operations. (Page 61)

Boney: The rock slate found embedded in a coal vein and considered an impurity that must be removed, or the weight of the coal will be docked by the weighmaster. (Page 61, 77)

Bootleg: Coal that is illegally mined for individual household use or sold by the miner without a royalty payment to the owner of the mining rights. (Page 34, 99)

Bottle coal: Very hard anthracite that sounds like glass bottles when chunks bump together. (Page 85)

Breaker: A large structure (figure 2) in which mined coal is prepared for retail sales by bringing it to the top with a conveyor line, and dropping it from one level to the next so the coal is crushed, screened to various sizes, and silt is washed away. (Page 34)

Cap piece: Wood wedge hammered above a prop to wedge the prop between mine floor and roof, as shown in figure 12. (Page 66)

Chamber: Underground room where the coal has been extracted. (Page 66)

Colliery: A mine employing a large number of miners, and usually, the site of a breaker, also. (Page 16)

Cutting coal: The practice of drilling coal with a precision that makes it a marketable size and blasts it to the most convenient position to load or scoop without causing a roof collapse. (Page 68)

Dead work: Work required to maintain the mine, other than mining coal. Examples are setting props, drilling a cut of coal, and gobbing rock. (Page 93)

Delays: Fuses set in sticks of dynamite to time detonations so that not all drill holes explode at the same time. (Page 68)

Dock: Weighmaster's reduction in the true weight of a truckload of coal as a penalty for coal that is of lesser quality than the quality that prevailed when the original sales price was set. (Page 62)

Doghole: Slang expression for a small underground mine employing few miners. (Page 10, 98)

Exploders: Fuses set in sticks of dynamite to set off the explosion as soon as the electric switch is thrown in the shanty. (Page 88)

Face: Wall of the vein to which mining has progressed and location where miners are working. (Page 62)

Gangway: The main tunnel where rails are in place for coal cars to be loaded and hoisted out to the tipple. (Page 60, 95, 96)

Grizzly: A mobile, vibrating piece of mining equipment used to reclaim, screen, and load fine anthracite coal from old waste dumps for sale to homes with stokers, or to electric generating stations. (Page 98)

Mary Ann: Slang for the equipment near a tipple that dumps mine cars full of rock into a truck. (Page 96)

Mucking: Moving water saturated soil or silt to get at the coal. (Page 89, 106)

Outcrop: The location where the deep vein of coal extends to the ground surface. (Page 9, 33, 96, 108)

Pinched vein: The natural thickness of a vein of coal is geologically reduced so that the miners are forced to work under extremely cramped quarters until the vein eventually returns to its natural height. (Page 66)

Props: Wood logs cut from area forests, then cut to size in the mine, and wedged between mine floor and roof to prevent roof collapse after the coal is removed. (Page 65, also see figure 12).

Robbing pillars: Period near end of a mine's life when remaining columns of coal are removed in their entirety, or nearly so. (Page 92)

Rib: Walls of the coal vein at the sides of the tunnel or chamber. (Page 109, also see figure 12).

Roll: A geological anomaly in a vein of coal where it abruptly terminates and reappears again some short distance away. (Page 109)

Royalty: Payment per ton by the small mining company to the legal owner of the mining rights to the coal mined. (Page 34)

Scabs: Slang expression given by miners to coworkers who continued mining coal after the majority of miners declared a strike for improved benefits. (Page 15)

Scoop: Slang expression for the steel bucket that drags about one ton of coal out of the mine. (Page 46, also see figure 7).

Soapstone: The accumulation of a thin film of soapy silt on the rock surface of a mine's roof as water seeps along the roof from tiny cracks. (Page 88)

Settlement: Name given to a small, usually remote, community 100–150 years ago where miners and their families settled around a large mine or colliery. (Page 19, 22)

Squeeze: Mine roof gradually settles as coal pillars are robbed or reduced in size. (Page 92)

Strip mine: Coal is mined by stripping away the overlaying soil and rock. (Page 60)

Tamping bags: Round paper tubes filled with coal dust and inserted in a drill hole after sticks of dynamite were inserted. The bags force the detonated dynamite to explode laterally into the coal, instead of back out the drill hole. (Page 68)

Tamping sticks: Used to ram the tamping bags into the drill hole after the dynamite sticks had been inserted. (Page 68)

Tipple: A large wood structure (also called a pocket) open at the top so coal cars on a sloping track could dump their loads, and trucks underneath could be loaded through a gate. Called tipple because in some variations, the coal cars were on horizontal tracks that could be tipped to dump their loads. (Page 60, also see figure 3).

Vein: A layer of coal, usually three to eight feet thick, and embedded between other layers of rock. (Page 85, also see figure 12).

Weighmaster: Technician at the breaker who manages the truck scale, reads the weight of the truck's load, applies any dockage, and issues a receipt to the driver. (Page 62)

X, Y, or Z license dump truck: The first letter on the license plate, denoting its size and legal highway weight limit. (Page 37, also see figure 4).

FOOTNOTES

1. "Stories from the Mines" presented by United Studios of America.
2. Gasperini, Aurora, Le Miniere di Lignite di Spoleto (1880-1960)

INDEX OF TOWNS AND PLACES

(See Figure 1 for Location Map)

Old Boston (P. 19, 25, 28, 29)
Old Forge (P. 62, 92, 94)
Pittston (P. 22, 25, 31, 121, 126)
Plains (P. 16, 19, 29)
Pottsville (P. 13)
Sebastapool (P. 27, 30, 113)
Small Dam (Gardner Creek Reservoir) (P. 75)
Spoleto, Italy (P. 16, 20)
Suscon (P. 49, 53, 107, 111)
Thornhurst (P. 116)
West Pittston (P. 85, 116)
West Virginia (P. 125)
Wilkes Barre (P. 13, 17)
Wyoming Valley (P. 10, 127)
Yatesville (P. 78, 93, 95, 108)

INDEX TO NAMES OF RELATIVES, FRIENDS, AND OTHERS

INDEX OF THE
LIST OF FIGURES

OTHER READING

I Remember Nonna, by August Carnevale, published by iUniverse, 2007.